The Best Of
sewing with
nancy ®

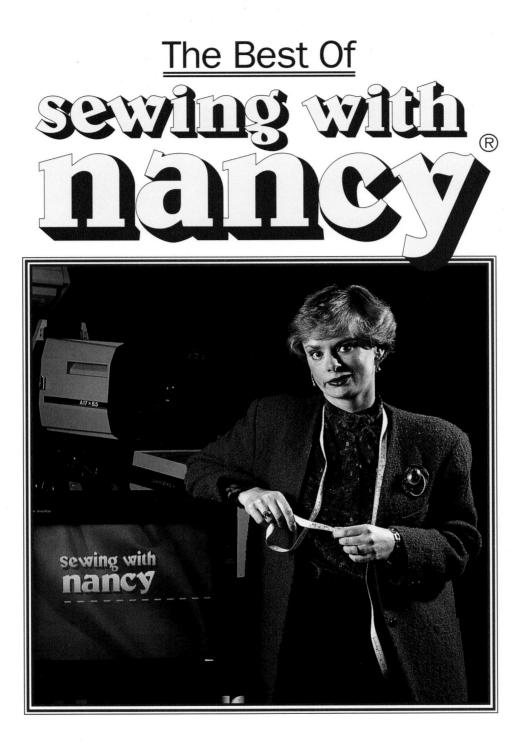

Nancy Zieman

The Best of Sewing With Nancy
©1993 by Oxmoor House, Inc.
Book Division of Southern Progress Corporation
P.O. Box 2463, Birmingham, Alabama 35201

Published by Oxmoor House, Inc., and Leisure Arts, Inc.

Library of Congress Number: 93-084933
Hardcover ISBN: 0-8487-1136-X
Softcover ISBN: 0-8487-1180-7
Manufactured in the United States of America
First Printing 1993

Editor-in-Chief: Nancy J. Fitzpatrick
Senior Crafts Editor: Susan Ramey Wright
Senior Editor, Editorial Services: Olivia Kindig Wells
Director of Manufacturing: Jerry Higdon
Art Director: James Boone

The Best of Sewing With Nancy

Editor: Carol Logan Newbill
Assistant Editor: Catherine S. Corbett
Editorial Assistant: Wendy L. Wolford
Copy Chief: Mary Jean Haddin
Assistant Copy Editor: L. Amanda Owens
Copy Assistant: Leslee Rester Johnson
Production Manager: Rick Litton
Associate Production Manager: Theresa L. Beste
Production Assistant: Marianne Jordan
Designer: Emily Albright
          Melinda Ponder Goode
Senior Photographer: John O'Hagan
Photographer: Ralph Anderson
Photostylists: Katie Stoddard, Karen Tindall Tillery

Illustrator: Rochelle Stibb
Editorial Assistance, Nancy's Notions: Susan Roemer
Dressmaking: Donna Fenske
             Phyllis Steinbach
             Nancy Zieman

Dedicated to all the loyal and supportive
Sewing With Nancy *viewers*
who tune in weekly
and give me the encouragement to keep on
sewing, serging, and quilting!

Thank you....

This book is named after my public television program. The first **Sewing With Nancy** *half-hour program was taped during the summer of 1982. Our living room served as the studio for this camera shoot, and the taping time for this one program totaled thirteen hours! After this humble beginning, never did I believe that I would be presenting* **Sewing With Nancy** *programs for eleven more years.*

The companies that supported this program during the past decade deserve my heartfelt thanks. Without their support, there would not be a TV program or, consequently, this book. **Pfaff Sewing Machines**, **Freudenberg/Pellon Nonwovens**, **Gingher, Inc.**, *and* **The McCall Pattern Co.** *have given me the green light to produce whatever sewing topics my staff and I feel will appeal to you. Again, I say "Thank you."*

I'd also like to extend a special thank you to the guests who have appeared on **Sewing With Nancy**. *Naomi Baker, Gail Brown, Gail Hamilton, Mary Mulari, Philip Pepper, and Jane Schenck have all enlightened my viewers with their sewing expertise.*

Contents

During the past 11 years, I have produced more than 286 Sewing With Nancy *television shows, sharing my favorite sewing techniques with viewers in the United States and Canada. From viewer mail and comments, I know which topics and series are your favorites—that's what you'll find in this book.*

There are five chapters, each like a book. For example, the "Speed Tailoring" chapter combines information that I presented in 11 TV programs. You'll find detailed, timesaving techniques on sewing a jacket in that one chapter. There'll be no need to refer to another book or to another chapter within this book; it will all be right there!

Let me know how you like The Best of Sewing With Nancy! *Your input helps me to help you sew!*

Happy sewing!
Nancy

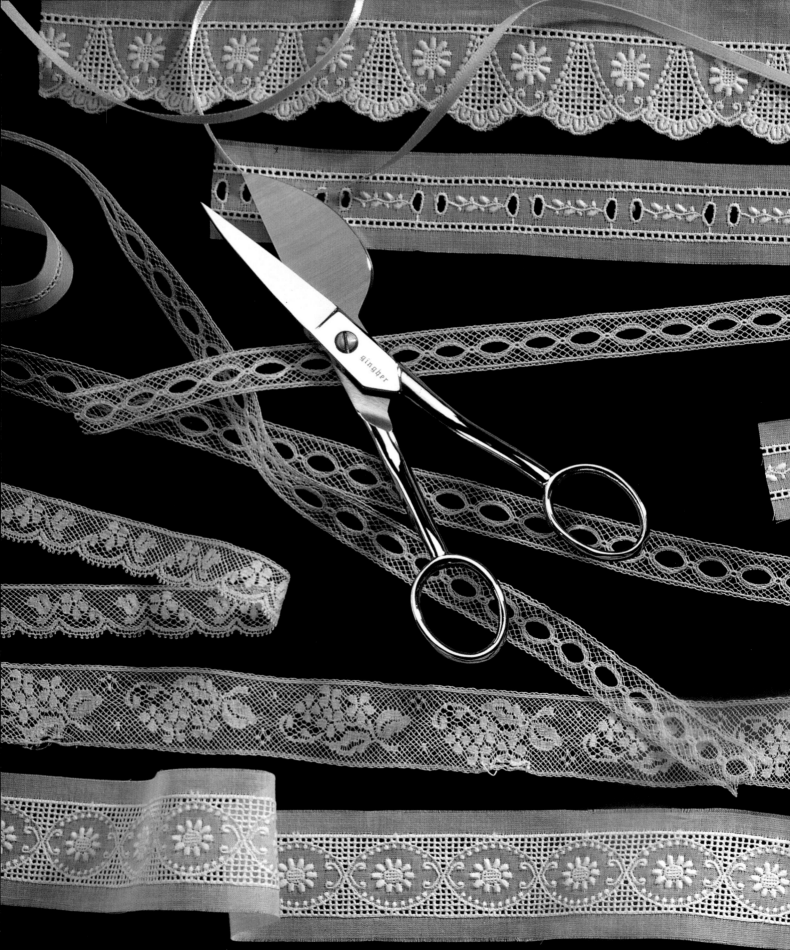

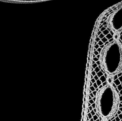
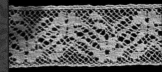

Sew
AN HEIRLOOM

Using a technique called French hand sewing to create beautiful garments and home decorating projects from fine fabrics and delicate laces and trims once took hours of handstitching. Those articles are true labors of love! You can achieve virtually the same effect in a much shorter time with a basic zigzag sewing machine. It's easy when you know how!

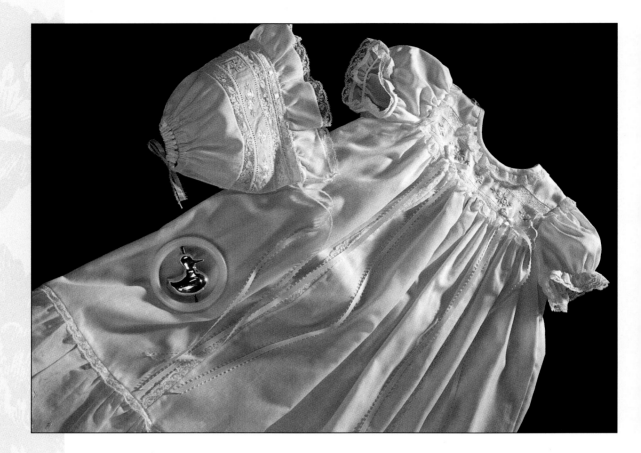

Gathering
THE PROJECT MATERIALS

Fabrics, Trims, and Laces

Fabrics

The type of fabric most commonly used for heirloom sewing is a lightweight, woven fabric called batiste, which may be 100% cotton or a blend of cotton and polyester. Heirloom garments and projects are generally made in white, ecru, or pastel colors.

Embroidered Trims

Catalogs and fabric stores have a wide assortment of Swiss embroideries, French laces, and trims. Each lace and trim has particular characteristics that influence how and where it should be used.

Entredeux (pronounced on-tra-doe), a French term meaning "between two," is the name given to a tightly woven, densely embroidered strip resembling a ladder. Because it is used to join two pieces of fabric, lace, or trim, entredeux is one of the most popular trims used for heirloom sewing. It is stitched on a 100% cotton batiste backing and is available in ⅛" and ¼" widths. After it is applied, only the embroidered "ladder" section is visible; the fabric on either side is included in the seam allowances or trimmed.

Swiss beading is a trim similar to entredeux. The main difference between the two is that beading has buttonhole-like openings wide enough to allow you to weave ⅛"- or ¼"-wide ribbon through the trim.

Swiss embroidery is a narrow strip of batiste, usually bordered by rows of entredeux on either side and decorated with delicate machine embroidery. Some types of Swiss embroidery, intended for use as edging on hemlines or sleeve edges, are finished with one scalloped edge.

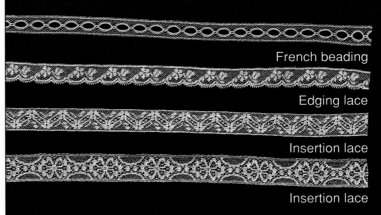

French beading is a special type of insertion lace. Like Swiss beading, it contains buttonhole-like openings for threading ribbon.

French beading
Edging lace
Insertion lace
Insertion lace

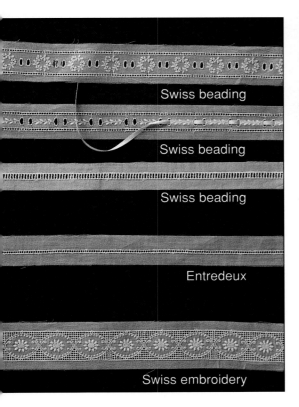

Swiss beading
Swiss beading
Swiss beading
Entredeux
Swiss embroidery

Laces

Because laces are not stitched onto a base fabric, they are generally less stable than embroidered trims. They also stretch more easily and have an appearance that is more delicate and open.

Along each straight edge, laces have a slightly heavier cord that can be pulled for gathering.

Insertion lace has two straight finished edges and is available in various widths and patterns. It can be inserted between two pieces of fabric or between other laces and trims.

Edging laces have one straight edge and one scalloped edge. Use edging lace for a decorative finish on hems, collars, necklines, cuffs, and ruffles.

Notions and Other Supplies

Here are some special supplies that will help make heirloom sewing faster and easier.

Needles

"Sharp" sewing machine needles, size 70 (9 American) or 80 (11 American), are recommended for general heirloom sewing. This type of needle, sometimes referred to as a "denim sharp" needle, has an extra-sharp point instead of the slightly rounded point found on a universal needle. A sharp needle pierces the fabric cleanly and produces a line of extremely straight stitching.

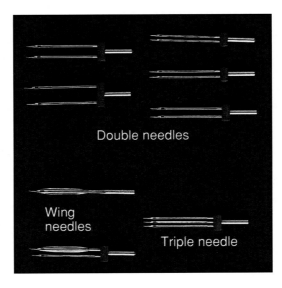

Double needles
Wing needles
Triple needle

Double needles, used for decorative effects and pintucks, fit any zigzag sewing machine that threads from front to back. A double needle consists of two needles mounted on a single needle shank. The two needles may be quite close together, or they may be farther apart.

Double needles are sized by a set of numbers such as "1.6/80." The number with the decimal point refers to the distance in millimeters between the two needles, while the second number refers to the size of each needle.

Double needles are available in five sizes. The first three sizes listed are commonly used for heirloom sewing. The other two sizes are usually reserved for sewing knits or for topstitching and decorative stitching.

Size:	Recommended for:
• 1.6/80	Heirloom sewing
• 2.0/80	Heirloom sewing
• 3.0/90	Heirloom sewing
• 4.0/90	Knits
• 6.0/100	Topstitching

Note from Nancy

Before you purchase a size 6.0/100 double needle, measure the opening on your sewing machine throat plate to make sure it's wide enough to accommodate this extra-wide double needle.

No matter what size double needle you choose, be sure to check the throat plate opening before you begin sewing by manually turning the balance wheel through one entire stitch. Decorative stitches often move the needle from side to side and the needle may hit the edge of the plate.

A double needle requires two threads on the top of the machine. As the machine stitches, the single bobbin thread moves back and forth between the two top threads, producing two lines of straightstitching on the right side of the fabric and a zigzag stitch on the wrong side.

Triple needles, which have three needles mounted on a crossbar with a single shaft, can be used only on zigzag machines that thread from the front to the back. Triple-needle stitching will multiply the beauty of straight or decorative sewing by producing three identical rows at once!

Wing needles, available only in size 100, are single needles with wide metal wings on either side. The needle's width produces distinct holes in the fabric as it stitches, resulting in a seam line that resembles entredeux.

Double wing needles combine one wing needle and one universal needle on a single shaft. Reserve this specialty needle for hemming or border stitching on heirloom projects.

Other Notions

The most suitable **thread** for delicate heirloom fabrics is one that closely matches the fabric's fiber content. For example, use 100% cotton thread on cotton batiste and all-purpose polyester/cotton thread on polyester/cotton blend fabrics.

Spray starch is essential for most heirloom projects. Starching and pressing before you stitch gives fabric, trims, and laces the additional body they need to remain smooth and flat during stitching.

Appliqué scissors are indispensable when creating heirloom garments. The pelican-shaped bill of this scissors makes it easier to trim the excess fabric close to a line of edgestitching without nicking the lace or trim. Position the rounded blade under the fabric and trim.

A **steam iron** is a sewing basic. Prior to starting your heirloom project, clean the bottom of the sole plate and rinse the water tank following the manufacturer's instructions. Delicate fabrics can easily be stained by the residues from a dirty iron.

A **puff iron,** so called because it is shaped specifically for pressing puffed sleeves and similar gathered pieces, provides a dual-temperature heated surface for pressing. (This is an optional ironing tool—one that is recommended if you've caught the "heirloom sewing bug.") This egg-shaped iron does not produce steam, and it presses even the most delicate fabrics without scorching. Attach the puff iron to the side of the sewing machine; then simply pass each completed seam over its heated surface. *(The surface is hot, so keep children away from the iron.)* This specialty iron is a real time-saver!

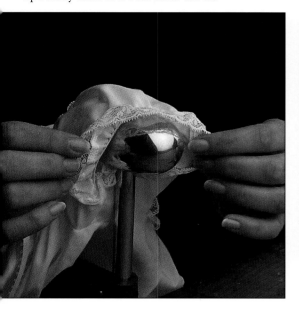

A *rotary cutter, ruler, and cutting mat* are perfect tools for heirloom sewing. The thick, transparent ruler makes it easy to roll the cutter along a straight edge. The cutting mat has 1" gridded lines to use as guides when straightening the fabric. The mat protects the table surface from the sharp blade.

Place the fabric on top of the specially designed cutting mat, align the ruler at the edge to be trimmed, and roll the cutter along the edge of the ruler to produce a sharp, accurately cut edge.

Stabilizers give support to delicate heirloom fabrics when you use decorative stitches. Look for brands such as Wash-Away (a water-soluble sheet), Perfect Sew (a water-soluble liquid), and nonwoven, removable fabrics like Totally Stable and Stitch-N-Tear.

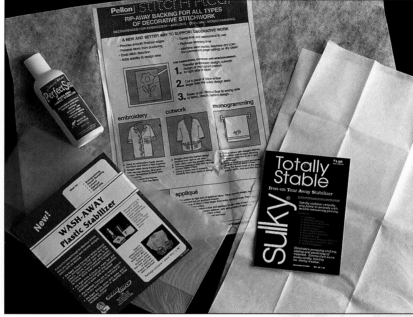

Marking tools with a non-oily base, such as quilting pencils and tailor's chalk, are recommended for marking heirloom garments. Blue or purple washable marking pens are great for general sewing but have a tendency to ghost (reappear as gray marks) after several years. Avoid using these pens when creating heirloom projects.

Mastering THE TECHNIQUES

Heirloom Basics

Speedy French Seams

A French seam is the perfect choice for joining garments made of delicate heirloom fabrics. With two rows of straightstitching and a little pressing, the raw edges of the fabric are encased attractively and neatly.

To join two garment pieces with a French seam:

1. With *wrong* sides together and raw edges aligned, straightstitch ⅜" from the cut edges.

2. Using a rotary cutter and cutting mat, trim the seam allowance to just slightly less than ¼".

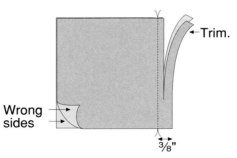

Wrong sides

←Trim.

⅜"

3. Press the joined edges flat and then press the seam open. This makes it easier to fold the seam allowance along the first stitching line in preparation for the second row of machine stitching.

4. Refold the seam allowance so that the *right* sides of the fabric are together, positioning the first stitching line at the fold. Stitch ¼" from the fold, encasing the cut edges to complete the French seam.

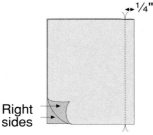

¼"

Right sides

Straightening the Fabric

With heirloom sewing, you'll be joining fabric to various lengths of laces and trims, so it is essential that your fabric be straight and perfectly on-grain. If the fabric is off-grain, it may pull and pucker, and your finished garment will not be as attractive. Here are two ways to straighten the fabric.

Pull-a-thread method—the preferred method:

1. Clip through the selvage and pull one of the threads. It's not usually necessary to completely remove the thread—pulling the thread even slightly creates a small pucker and provides a guide for cutting.

2. Cut along the pulled-thread line with a rotary cutter or shears. Once the fabric has been straightened by this method, subsequent cuts can be made by measuring from the straight edge and then cutting.

Selvage

Selvage

Clip-and-tear method:

1. Clip through the selvage and tear across the width of the fabric.

2. Trim the edges with a ruler, rotary cutter, and cutting mat.

This technique usually works best on polyester/cotton batiste. On some fabrics, however, the torn edge is excessively fluted. Try this technique on a scrap first to see if it is a suitable method for the fabric you are using.

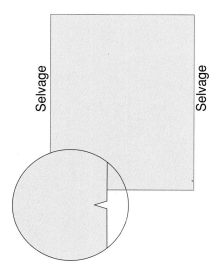

Applying Entredeux

Applying entredeux between two pieces of fabric is a basic heirloom sewing technique. Here's how to easily add entredeux to any project.

1. Cut the fabric and the entredeux to the same length. Spray-starch and press both the trim and the fabric.

2. Set the sewing machine for a straight-stitch with a medium stitch length (12 stitches per inch).

3. With the right sides of the entredeux and the fabric or trim together, straightstitch next to the well of the entredeux (approximately a ¼" seam). This positions the entredeux.

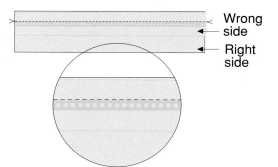

Wrong side
Right side

4. Press or finger-press the seam allowances away from the entredeux so that the embroidery openings are visible.

> ### Note from Nancy
> Sometimes I finger-press a seam to save time. Fold the fabric where desired, slip the fold between your thumb and index finger, and press together. This produces a temporary crease.

5. Set the sewing machine for a zigzag stitch of medium length and width.

6. Working from the right side, zigzag the seam flat. Guide the edge of the entredeux down the center of the foot so that the "zig" is in the fabric and the "zag" is in the hole of the entredeux. One stitch should form in the center of each entredeux hole. Fine-tune the stitch width and length to the size of the entredeux.

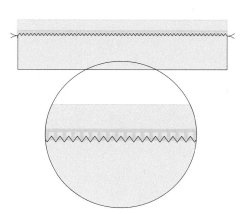

7. Trim the seam allowances with an appliqué scissors. Or use a conventional shears and bevel the blades by holding them flat against the fabric as you trim.

Applying Insertion Laces with a Rolled Stitch

With this technique, you can attach insertion laces and finish the raw edges of your fabric, all in one step. The cut edge of the fabric rolls over the edge of the lace during stitching.

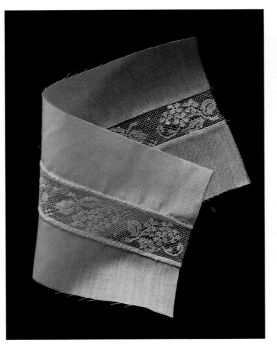

1. Spray-starch the laces and fabric; press.
2. Adjust the machine for a wide zigzag stitch and a short stitch length.
3. Place the right sides of the lace and the fabric together. With the lace on top, extend the fabric ⅛" to the right of the lace.
4. Insert the needle in the edge of the lace. Stitch, with the "zig" catching the lace edge and the "zag" passing over the extended fabric, causing it to roll over the lace.

5. Press the seam allowance toward the fabric.

6. Working from the right side, edgestitch along the pressed seam allowance.

7. Repeat for the second side of the insertion lace.

Gathering and Joining Edging Lace to Fabric

Gathered edging lace is often added to collars, sleeves, or hemlines. The gathered lace may be attached to entredeux or directly to the batiste.

1. Cut the edging lace twice as long as the fabric to which it will be joined. For example: for fabric 24" long, cut 48" of lace.
2. Quarter-mark both the lace and the fabric, marking the quarters with pins.

> ### Note from Nancy
> *I find quarter marking a quick and accurate way to evenly distribute fabric. Fold the lace in half and insert a pin at the fold. Fold the lace in half again and insert pins at each new fold. Repeat for the fabric. Then match the quarter marks on the lace to those on the fabric and pin the lace to the fabric.*

3. To gather the lace, find the cord on the straight edge of the lace and pull.

4. With the right sides of the lace and the fabric together, align the quarter marks and extend the fabric ⅛" beyond the edge of the lace.

5. Adjust the gathers evenly.

> **Note from Nancy**
> I sometimes use a tweezers to help adjust and position the gathers as I sew. The tweezers will allow you to control the gathers without getting your fingers in the way. You can always see exactly what you're doing.

6. Join the lace to the fabric using a rolled stitch with a wide zigzag and short stitch length. The batiste should roll over the edge of the gathered lace.

7. Finger-press the seam allowance toward the fabric. Working from the right side, topstitch along the seam.

Joining Lace to Lace

Create an open, airy section of heirloom fabric by joining lace to lace. Because laces usually have a repetitive design, the placement of the designs must be considered prior to sewing. When you sew identical laces together, stack or stagger the designs. (Staggering the designs is much easier to match and is equally as attractive.)

1. Spray-starch and press the laces.

2. Adjust the sewing machine for a zigzag stitch of medium width and short to medium length.

3. Butt the edges of the laces together, carefully positioning the lace designs as desired.

4. Zigzag the laces together.

> **Note from Nancy**
> To prevent the delicate laces from being drawn into the feed dogs, begin sewing ¼" to ½" from the cut ends. Also grasp the thread tails and hold them firmly behind the presser foot until the lace begins to feed through the machine.

17

Timesaving Notions
If the laces you are using are especially delicate and tend to stretch despite starching, back the laces with Wash-Away, a water-soluble stabilizer.

• *Position a piece of Wash-Away slightly larger than the laces on one half of a non-stick appliqué pressing sheet.*

• *Place the laces on the Wash-Away, butting the long edges of the laces.*

• *Fold the pressing sheet over the laces and press. This temporarily fuses the laces to the Wash-Away and provides a more stable working surface.*

• *Peel the fused laces from the pressing sheet and stitch as usual.*

• *Remove the Wash-Away by tearing away the large sections and spritzing water on the remaining scraps.*

Joining Lace to Entredeux

Joining lace to entredeux is a new sewing challenge because the lace has a finished edge and the entredeux has a seam allowance. The challenge is easily met by trimming the batiste edge on the entredeux. This unconventional sewing technique is possible because the entredeux edge does not ravel!

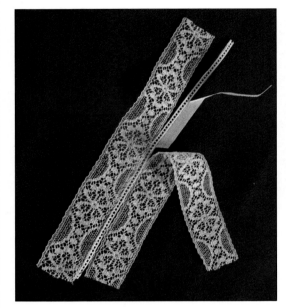

1. Trim the fabric seam allowance from the entredeux. Trim as closely as possible to prevent "whiskers" (raveled threads) from showing on the completed project.

2. Spray-starch and press both the lace and the entredeux.

3. Butt the edge of the lace to the trimmed edge of the entredeux.

4. Zigzag the lace and the entredeux together with a stitch of medium width and short length. The "zig" of the stitch should fall in the lace and the "zag" in the hole of the entredeux.

5. Repeat for the second side of the lace.

Combining Steps

Now that you know the basics of working with laces and trims, it's time to design and create your own heirloom garment.

Note from Nancy
When I first started doing heirloom sewing, I was intimidated by the thought of positioning and joining the various trims and laces. I believed it would be difficult to determine what to place where and when. But once you get started, it's not difficult at all. Begin with your favorite lace or trim as the center and build upon the design by adding whatever lace or trim combinations appeal to you.

1. Determine the arrangement of the laces and trims.

2. Consider the degree of stretch of the laces and trims you are using. Cut laces and trims 1" to 2" longer than needed. This allows room for slight variation in elasticity as the laces are joined. The raw ends of the completed piece can be trimmed after all the stitching is completed.

3. Organize the trims and laces on a terry towel in the order in which they will be sewn. Roll the trims in the towel and place it next to the sewing machine.

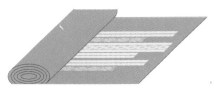

4. Join the various laces and trims, working in sequence from left to right and following the techniques previously detailed. If you're unable to complete all the sewing at one time, or if you are interrupted as you sew, it's easy to roll up the towel so that the trims remain neat and in the correct order until it's time to sew again!

5. If your fabric includes beading, you may wish to weave ribbon through the beading as an accent.

6. After all the laces and trims are joined, trim the ends to square the fabric or cut the pattern piece from the joined lace.

Texturizing Fabric

Heirloom sewing is not limited to working with laces and trims. The term also refers to changing the texture and appearance of fabric with delicate stitching or gathering techniques. Here are several ways to add elegant heirloom effects to your garments.

Making Puffing Strips

Puffing strips are easy-to-sew dimensional accents that can be incorporated into an heirloom project. These strips are made by gathering both long edges of a batiste strip, creating a "puffed" strip of fabric. The strip is then joined to other heirloom laces and trims.

1. Cut the batiste strips on the crosswise grain (from selvage to selvage), twice the length needed for the finished puffing strip. Suggested strip widths are 1½" to 3" wide.

2. Gather the edges of each strip.

• Grasp both the top and bobbin sewing machine threads to form the gathering threads. Pull the threads the full length of the batiste strip and slightly twist the threads together.

• Position the threads along one edge of the strip, allowing a ⅛" margin between the edge of the fabric and the threads. Stitch, using a zigzag stitch of medium width and short length, with the "zig" in the fabric and the "zag" off the fabric edge. As the gathering threads are encased, the edge of the puffing strip is also finished, preventing raveling.

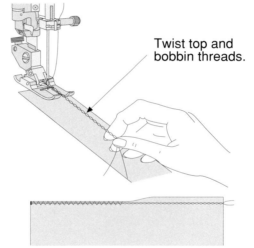

Twist top and bobbin threads.

• Turn the strip over; pull and twist a second set of threads. Position those threads along the remaining edge of the strip and stitch as before. (You will be stitching along one edge from the right side of the fabric and along the other edge from the wrong side.) Both lines of zigzagging will be secured at the same end of the puffing strip, while both free ends of the gathering threads will be on the opposite end.

Timesaving Notions
A double-eyed needle makes it easy to thread ribbons through heirloom beading and laces. Thread the ribbon through the needle, insert the needle in the lace, and pull the ribbon through.

• Pull both gathering threads at the same time to uniformly space the gathers. Gather to the finished size.

3. Pin the puffing strips to the ironing board, adjusting gathers evenly. Steam to set the gathers. Allow the strips to dry thoroughly after steaming.

Timesaving Notions
A blindhem or topstitching foot has an adjustable guide bar that acts as a perfect guide when stitching uniform tucks. When the fabric fold is positioned along the foot's guide bar, every tuck is the same distance from the fabric fold.

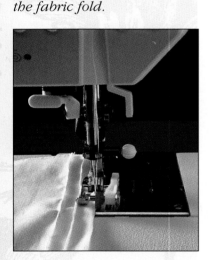

Note from Nancy
Avoid resting the weight of the iron on the gathers. The object is to set the gathers so that they remain evenly spaced, not to flatten them.

4. Attach lace or trim to either side of the puffing strip and continue with the project.

Stitching Crossover Tucks

Tucks on a collar or yoke add subtle texture to blouses, dresses, and children's wear. The look is more tailored than the feminine touches of laces and trims, yet it blends well with other heirloom effects. Best of all, the sewing is simple!

1. Cut the fabric to be tucked 2" to 4" wider and longer than the finished collar or yoke pattern, since the tucks will take up some of the fabric's width and length.

2. Mark the vertical and the horizontal tuck placement lines 1" to 1½" apart, using an oil-free quilting pencil or tailor's chalk.

3. Replace the machine foot with a blind-hem or topstitching foot.

4. With *wrong* sides together, fold and press the fabric along the vertical placement lines. Stitch the vertical tucks ¼" from fold, guiding the fabric folds along the foot's guide.

5. Press the tucks in one direction.

Press tucks.

Note from Nancy
Use lots of steam when pressing! Batiste handles much better when you use sufficient steam. If you find the fabric lacks body after steam pressing, give it a shot of spray starch and re-press before you continue sewing.

6. Stitch the crosswise tucks, stitching all rows in the same direction as the first tucks were pressed. (It's like working with napped fabric. If all rows are not stitched in the same direction, the presser foot may force some tucks in one direction, while others face in the opposite direction.)

7. Press the stitched tucks, beginning at one corner and pressing all in the same direction.

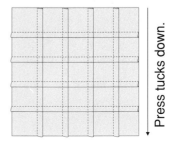

Press tucks down.

8. Add a decorative machine stitch in the center of selected "windowpanes" for an artistic accent.

Creating Heirloom Embroidery

Although there are numerous beautiful laces and trims on the market, sometimes it's fun to make a trim that is uniquely yours. Use your sewing machine's decorative stitch capabilities to make an embroidered trim and include that trim in your next heirloom project. It's quick and easy, and the trim can be personalized even more by your choice of threads.

• Cut a batiste strip slightly longer than needed for the embroidery. Mark the fabric by pressing it lightly to indicate the stitching line, or mark with a washable pencil.

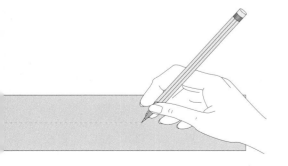

• Back the stabilizer with a water-soluble stabilizer, a nonwoven stabilizer, or saturate with a liquid stabilizer.

• Stitch along the marked line with a decorative stitch. Remove the stabilizer.

Batiste

Stabilizer

• Join the embroidery to other heirloom laces and trims and continue with your project.

Sewing Heirlooms with the Double Needle

A common embellishment seen on many heirloom garments is rows and rows of perfectly straight, perfectly stitched pintucks. It's easy to make pintucks if you use a double needle. But double needles are not just for pintucks! This section contains many innovative ways of creating charming heirloom designs with a double needle.

Double-Needle Pintucks

Keeping pintucks absolutely straight used to be a difficult task. With the help of a double needle and a pintuck foot, that obstacle is a thing of the past.

1. Pull a thread slightly to provide a line for guiding the stitching for the first row of pintucking.

2. To set up your machine:

• The double needle requires a separate thread for each needle's eye. Place a second spool of matching thread on the extra spool pin or wind a bobbin with the same thread to use as the second needle thread.

• Following the threading instructions for your machine, guide both threads as one through the tension disk and thread guides. At the needles, separate the threads and insert one thread through the eye of each needle.

Timesaving Notions
Perfect Sew is a liquid stabilizer that adds crispness and firmness to the fabric and then washes away. Just apply it to the fabric, dry with a hair dryer, and stitch. I feel confident using this product—it is nontoxic, non-allergenic, and environmentally safe.

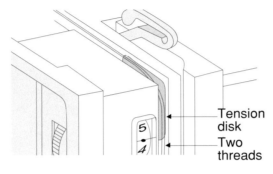

Tension disk
Two threads

• Replace the conventional presser foot with a pintuck foot. The pintuck foot has a series of grooves, or channels, on the underside of the foot. The foot may contain five to nine grooves, depending on the particular manufacturer.

• Slightly tighten the upper tension to make the pintucks "tuck."

3. To stitch the tucks:

• Position the needles along the marked stitching line and stitch the first pintuck.

• After completing the first row of pin-tucking, align that row in one of the grooves on the pintuck foot. The groove selected determines the distance between the rows of pintucks.

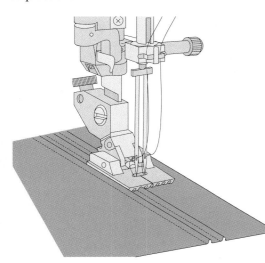

• Stitch all rows in the same manner, always positioning the previously stitched row in that same groove of the pintuck foot.

Pintucks in the Round

If you're stitching an area with multiple rows of pintucks (for example, the front of a garment or a collar or cuffs), here's a way to reduce the amount of time needed for stitching. Instead of stitching each tuck individually and cutting threads after each row, sew all the tucks with one continuous line of stitching.

1. Cut the fabric a few inches longer than needed for the project. (The ends of the fabric will be trimmed after the stitching is completed.) Straighten the fabric.

2. Pull a thread, press-mark, or mark a line on the fabric to act as a guide for the first row of stitching.

3. Mark the starting point for the second row of stitching ¼" away from the first marked line.

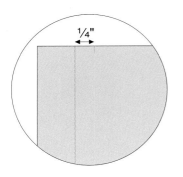

4. Align the end of the first marked row with the start of the second marked row. Slightly overlap the two ends of the fabric to make a tube.

5. Stitch the ends together, making certain the tube is large enough to fit around the free arm of the sewing machine.

6. Place the tube, right side out, under the presser foot, positioning the needles along the marked line. The majority of the fabric should be positioned to the right of the presser foot. Bring up the bobbin thread, pull it to the top side, and draw the threads to the back of the machine.

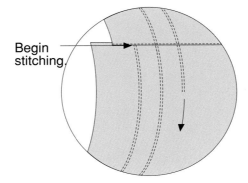

Begin stitching

7. Stitch along the first marked line, holding the fabric taut. At the end of the row, the needles will align with the second row to be pintucked. Guide the first stitched row into a groove on the pintuck foot.

8. Continue stitching around the tube, completing all pintucks.

9. Remove the tube from the machine. Cut the fabric apart at the original seam line.

Corded Pintucks

For a more defined, raised effect and slightly firmer pintucks, add cording as you stitch the tucks.

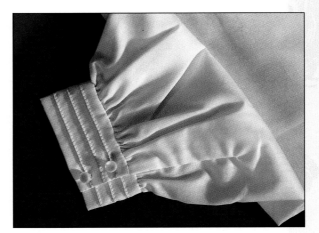

Timesaving Notions
To quickly thread the cording through the machine throat plate, I use my Serger Looper and Needle Threader. Insert the curved end of the threader through the circular opening in the top of the throat plate, loop the cording through the wire end, and pull the cording up through the opening.

1. Use #8 pearl cotton thread, topstitching thread, or a similar cording thread.

> **Note from Nancy**
> *I often like to select cording a shade darker than the fabric. The darker cording adds a shadow effect to the completed pintucks.*

2. Thread the cording through the opening in the machine throat plate. Leave the bobbin area open so that the cording can flow freely through the machine as the pitucks are stitched.

3. Stitch the pintucks as previously described. The cording is fed from the underside of the machine and secured as the bobbin thread zigzags between the two needle threads.

Pintuck Smocking

Pintuck smocking is completed using a combination of machine pintucks and hand smocking. A contrasting or coordinating thread, such as ribbon floss, pearl cotton, or embroidery floss, can be used for the hand stitching.

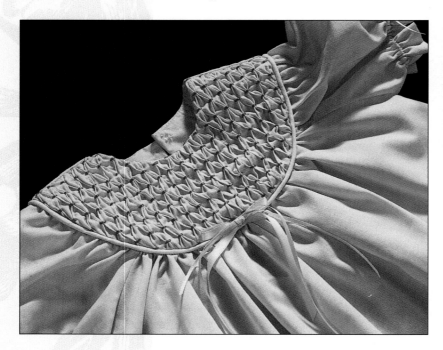

• Determine the amount of fabric needed by multiplying the pattern width by 2½. For example: if the pattern width is 10", multiply 10" by 2½ to equal 25" of fabric needed.
• Mark the fabric at ½" intervals with a marking pencil or chalk.

• Stitch rows of pintucks following the ½" marks.
• Mark across the pintucks horizontally at ½" intervals.
• Handstitch or smock at alternate marks, stitching two rows of pintucking together. First, catch the width of the pintuck twice; then go under the pintuck to the far side of the next pintuck and repeat.
• Finish smocking the entire piece. Cut out the pattern from the smocked piece of fabric.

Double-Needle Shadow Embellishments

Shadow Borders

Embellish a hemline with a shadow border. This subtle effect is created with a double needle, a scalloped stitch, and a layer of contrasting "shadow" fabric.

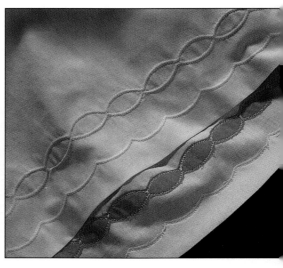

1. Select a brightly colored solid fabric (cotton or polyester/cotton blend) for the shadow fabric. Prewash the fabric to make certain the color does not bleed.

> **Note from Nancy**
> *I like to check the effect of the fabric combinations by placing the shadow fabric under one layer of batiste. In general, the brighter the color, the better, because the batiste will diffuse the color. The effect can be varied by adjusting the intensity of the shadow fabric and/or the number of layers of surface fabric covering it. The decision is yours!*

2. Cut the shadow fabric 2" wide. Place the shadow fabric behind the batiste. Pin in place.

3. To set up your machine:

• Insert a size 2.0/80 or 3.0/90 double needle.

• Set the machine for a decorative scallop outline stitch. Turn the balance wheel by hand or run the machine slowly to make sure the needle won't hit the foot or plate.

4. Stitch the design, beginning at a side seam. (One half of the shadow border is created by one row of scallop stitching.) Stop with the needle in the raised position.

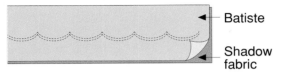

Batiste

Shadow fabric

5. Lift the presser foot and rotate the fabric. Lower the presser foot, repositioning the left needle in the last hole made by the right needle. Stitch the second half of the design. (Rotating the fabric and placing the needle in the last sewn stitch creates a "mirror image" of the scallop during the second stitching. This enables both sides of the design to line up with the motifs meeting in the centers.)

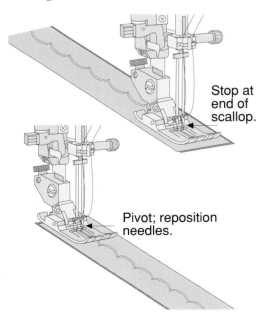

Stop at end of scallop.

Pivot; reposition needles.

6. Use an appliqué scissors (or bevel a regular scissors) to trim excess shadow fabric from both sides of the stitched design. Press.

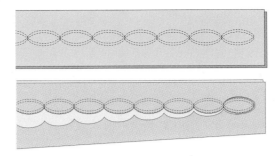

Shadow Border Hems

Continue the same scalloped shadow effect as a hemming element. This heirloom technique produces an attractive hem for children's garments.

1. Turn up the hem and press.

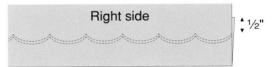

Right side

½"

2. Scallop-stitch around the hem, working from the right side of the fabric, ½" from the cut edge.

3. Turn the garment to the wrong side. Trim the hem allowance that extends beyond the scallop stitching. (Trimming is the key element in achieving the shadow effect.) Use an appliqué scissors, or bevel the blades of a scissors, to cut close to the stitching.

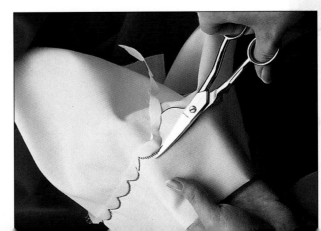

Timesaving Notions

Timesaving Notions
A nonwoven, iron-on stabilizer like Totally Stable is an ideal product to use for the pillowcase technique. The product has a light fusible coating that bonds to the fabric when pressed, yet doesn't leave a gummy residue after the stabilizer is removed.

Timesaving Notions
Check your accessory box for an appliqué foot. The underside of this foot has a hollowed or grooved section, providing space for satin stitching to flow easily through the machine. (On some machines, this foot may be called an open toe or embroidery foot.)

Creating with Novelty Needles

Wing, double wing, and triple needles are truly novelty needles that can best be featured in heirloom sewing. Try this simple pillowcase to showcase these stitches. It's a perfect wedding or shower gift!

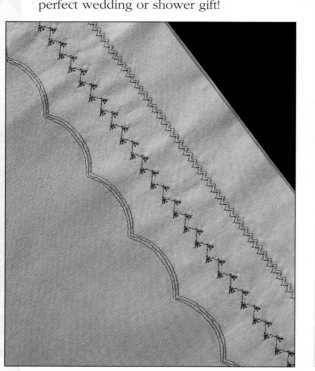

1. For each pillowcase, cut a rectangle of fabric measuring 44" x 36".

2. Fold the rectangle in half with right sides together, aligning the edges. Serge or sew the top and side of the pillowcase, using a ¼" seam allowance.

3. Fold a 4" hem along the open edge; press.

4. Stiffen and support the fabric by spraying it with spray starch and then pressing. Back the hem allowance with a stabilizer such as Totally Stable.

5. Insert a triple needle, threading each needle with its own thread.

6. Stitch the hem, using a scalloped or straight stitch. Trim the excess hem allowance with an appliqué scissors.

7. Change to a wing needle. Select a decorative stitch that has an open pattern. Stitch.

8. Change to a double wing needle. Select a straight stitch or a narrow zigzag pattern. Stitch.

Decorating with Ornamental Stitches

Machine Bridging

Add delicate lacy accents to christening gowns, children's garments, blouses, or dresses with this unique sewing machine technique. The key to this easy treatment lies in combining a delicate feather stitch with two specialty presser feet: an appliqué foot and a pintuck foot.

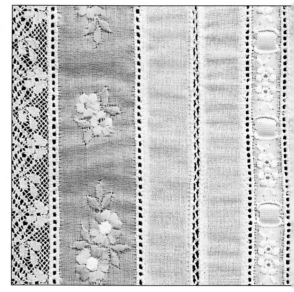

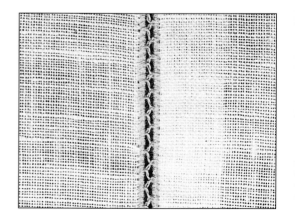

1. Attach an appliqué foot.

2. Set the machine for a narrow zigzag with a short stitch length.

3. Fold under the ⅝" seam allowance on each of the fabric edges to be joined with machine bridging.

4. Position a length of pearl cotton or topstitching thread along the fold of one of the fabric pieces. Zigzag the thread to the fold.

The "zig" should catch the fabric fold while the "zag" goes off the fabric, couching the thread. Repeat along the edge of the second fabric piece.

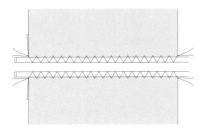

5. Attach a 7-groove pintuck foot. Place one corded edge to the left of the foot's center groove and the second corded edge to the right of the center.

6. Stitch, using your machine's decorative feather stitch. The feather stitch bridges, or joins, the two fabric pieces.

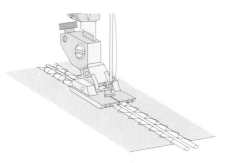

7. Trim the excess seam allowances from the wrong side of the fabric. (Because the edge is overcast with the zigzag stitches, the fabric will not ravel.)

Off-the-edge Scallops

For another creative application, add off-the-edge scallops. Use the scallops as a delicate, lacy edge finish or as a unique inset.

1. To set up the machine:
- Thread #5 pearl cotton through the hole in the sewing machine throat plate.
- Set the machine for a scallop stitch with a satin-stitch length slightly shorter than generally recommended. A shorter stitch length provides better coverage for the decorative stitching.
- Set the tension at buttonhole setting. For most machines, this is two settings lower than normal stitching.

2. To stitch the scallops:
- Work on the folded edge of the fabric.
- Place a strip of a nonwoven stabilizer, such as Stitch-N-Tear, under the fold to stabilize the edge.

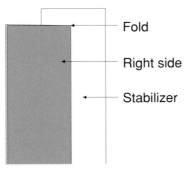

Fold

Right side

Stabilizer

- Place the first stitch of the scallop in the fabric fold. Only the ends of the scallop fall on the fabric; the remainder of the scallop is stitched on the stabilizer.

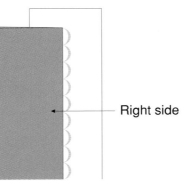

Right side

• Stitch without placing tension on the fabric. If the fabric is held taut, it tightens the pearl cotton and flattens the scallops. Relax as you stitch!

3. After completing the stitching, gently remove the stabilizer. Pulling too hard could tear the scallops from the fabric edge.

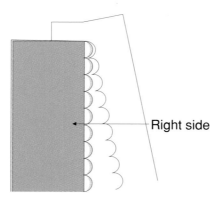

Right side

Scallop Bridging

For a dramatic insert, try scallop bridging—two fabric edges finished with sewing machine scallops and then joined with bar tacks.

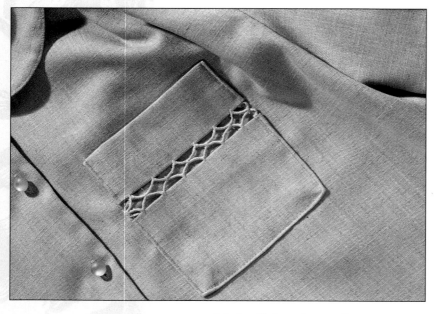

• Stitch off-the-edge scallops on two fabric edges, following the previous instructions.

• Butt the scallops together, aligning the centers of each scallop.

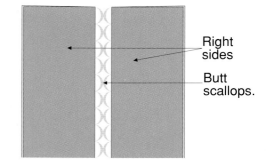

Right sides

Butt scallops.

• Join the centers of two scallops by machine bar tacking (or use the button sew-on stitch). Advance to the next set of scallops and bar tack. Repeat until all the sets are joined.

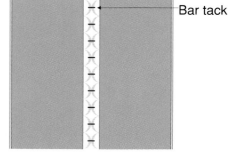

Bar tack

Serging an Heirloom

For those of you who own sergers, heirloom projects can be sewn quickly and creatively with rolled-edge, overlock, or flatlock stitches instead of conventional sewing. For example, use your serger to gather the edges of puffing strips or use the flatlock stitch to attach ribbon.

This section contains basic heirloom shortcuts for your serger. Feel free to use a serger in tandem with a conventional machine to develop your own serger accents.

Rolled-Edge Pintucks

1. Set the serger for a narrow rolled-edge stitch. Use a decorative thread such as machine embroidery thread in the upper looper.

2. Mark the fabric at 1" intervals with a marking pen.

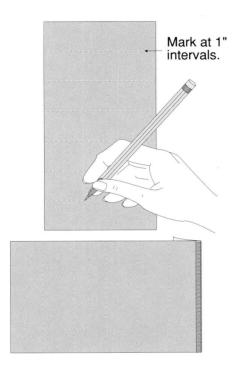

Mark at 1"
intervals.

3. With wrong sides together, fold the fabric along the 1" marking lines.

4. Slip the fabric under the presser foot and serge. Guide the fabric away from the serger blade so that the fold of the fabric is not cut as you serge. Disengage the blade, if possible.

Insertion Lace with a Serger

Instead of applying insertion lace to fabric with a rolled stitch at the sewing machine, try using a rolled-edge stitch on the serger for a neater finish. As an option, the stitches could be exposed for an additional decorative effect.

With right sides together, serge the two layers together with a rolled-edge stitch. The end result looks the same as application with a conventional sewing machine—the added benefit is that you spend less time stitching!

Applying Entredeux with a Serger

Another heirloom sewing option to try combines sewing machine and serger techniques.

1. Cut the fabric and the entredeux to the same length and spray-starch both pieces.

2. With the right sides of the entredeux and the fabric together, straightstitch next to the well of the entredeux stitching. Press the seam allowances away from the entredeux so that the holes are visible.

3. After completing the initial straight-stitching, serge the raw edges with a rolled-edge stitch. This eliminates the zigzag stitching and trimming necessary with conventional stitching.

Serger Gathering

The basic 3/4-thread overlock stitch can quickly and accurately gather puffing strips. The secret is in changing the needle tensions.

1. Adjust the serger for a 3/4-thread overlock stitch. Tighten both needle threads to the tightest setting.

2. Serge each edge of the puffing strip. The fabric will automatically gather and the edges will be finished with a narrow rolled-edge, all in one operation.

Quilted Fashions
& MORE!

Quilting can be used for much more than bed coverings. If you learn to think of quilting as an accent or embellishment instead of a project in itself, you will begin to see the many ways you can incorporate small quilted details into garments and home decorating projects. It's the perfect opportunity to introduce yourself to this distinctive art form.

Checklist for Selecting
Fabric Colors for Garments:
Who is going to wear it?
What are the person's hair color and skin
tone?
What are his or her favorite colors?
What shades does the person prefer—
darker? lighter?

Understanding Basic Quilting Techniques

Most of the quilting projects in this chapter depend on the basics of cutting, stitching, and pressing. Let's look at the general guidelines for quilting.

Cutting the Fabric

Before you cut, prewash all your fabrics. Prewashing removes the sizing and makes the fabric easier to handle, helps prevent skipped stitches, and eliminates the possibility of shrinkage after the project is completed. It isn't necessary to wash a full cycle; a short cycle with a small amount of detergent works just as well.

The quilting techniques in this chapter are based on cutting strips of fabric and joining them in various ways. By far the quickest and easiest way to cut strips is to use a rotary cutter, ruler, and cutting mat.

To cut strips using rotary cutting tools:

1. Fold the fabric as it comes from the bolt, with wrong sides together and selvages aligned. If you are right-handed, place the majority of the fabric to your right, as shown in the diagram. If you are left-handed, place the majority of the fabric to the left.

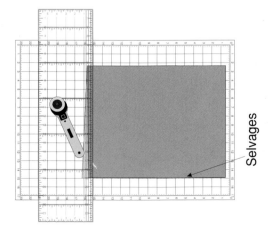

Selvages

Choosing Fabrics for Quilting

One of the most crucial parts of any quilting project is selecting fabrics. Although 100% cotton fabrics are most often used for making traditional bed quilts, blends of cotton/polyester can also be used successfully in most of these projects.

Be sure the fabrics you choose are compatible in weight. (If you absolutely fall in love with one fabric that is lighter in weight than the others, fuse a light interfacing such as Pellon Featherweight to the wrong side to add body.) If possible, try to use fabrics that are similar in fiber content—use all-cotton fabrics together or choose similar blends of cotton and polyester. Mixing fabrics of different fiber content, which often require different pressing temperatures, can cause difficulties in block construction.

Don't forget to consider colors when choosing fabrics for quilted garments. Use this checklist to help you plan your choices.

2. Square the raw edge of the fabric closest to you by aligning the selvage edges along one of the mat's horizontal markings. Align a ruler along the vertical marking closest to the crosswise edge of the fabric. Trim along that marking with the rotary cutter.

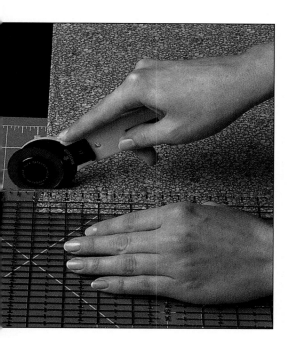

3. With the selvages aligned along one of the mat's horizontal markings, measure the desired width of the strip. Place a ruler at the mark and cut along the ruler with the rotary cutter. Repeat to cut the desired number of strips.

Setting Up Your Sewing Machine

Although quilting uses many of the same techniques as fashion sewing, there are a few differences you should note when piecing quilt strips.

1. Use all-purpose sewing thread in a neutral color or a color that blends with your fabric. For best results, use the same type of thread in both the needle and the bobbin.

2. Set the stitch length at 15 stitches per inch. Because the stitching is not locked at the beginning and end of each seam, as usual in fashion sewing, the shorter stitch length makes the stitching more secure.

3. In quilting, all seams are stitched with ¼" seam allowances, unless otherwise specified. Here are several ways to control the width of the seam allowance:

• Use the right edge of the presser foot as a stitching guide, provided it is exactly ¼" from the needle. Or measure ¼" from the needle and mark the presser foot at that position.

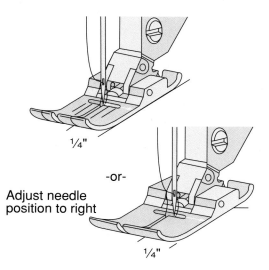

Adjust needle position to right

• Adjust the position of the needle so that it is precisely ¼" from the edge of the presser foot. This is possible on some, but not all, machines.

Setting Up Your Serger

Because your serger can easily stitch a finished ¼" seam, it is a great way to stitch quilting projects.

To set up your serger for quilting:

1. Use a 3/4-thread overlock stitch and all-purpose serger thread.

2. Adjust the stitch-width dial so that the distance between the left needle and the cut edge of the fabric is ¼".

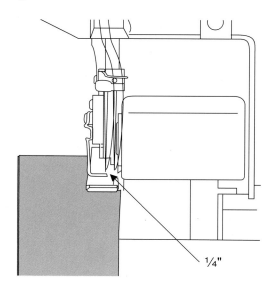

Timesaving Notions

Stitching precise, uniform seam allowances is extremely important; it helps assure that all the finished squares will be the same size. The Little Foot, a presser foot designed for quilters, has a right edge that is exactly ¼" from the needle and is notched ¼" in front of and behind the center needle position—the perfect reference for starting, stopping, and pivoting.

The Little Foot fits most standard low-shank machines with a center needle and straight stitch. It also fits some slant-needle and high-shank machines. Consult your dealer to find out whether the Little Foot will fit your machine.

Continuous or Chain Piecing

When joining several identical sets of strips for a quilted project, continuous or chain piecing can be used to save time.

1. With right sides together and raw edges aligned, join the first two strips of fabric. Do not raise the presser foot or clip the threads at the end of the seam.

2. Take two more strips of the same colors and place them with right sides together and raw edges aligned. Butt the second pair of strips against the first pair of stitched strips and continue stitching.

3. In the same fashion, join all of the strips so that the pairs are connected by a chain of threads.

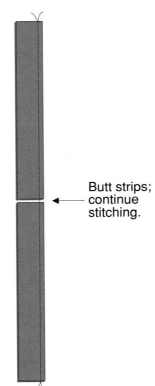

Butt strips; continue stitching.

4. When all of the strips are stitched, clip the threads between sets.

Pressing

Just as in fashion sewing, pressing is critical to the success of projects featuring quilted accents. Follow these general pressing guidelines to help maintain sharp seams and flat, smooth blocks.

• Use an up-and-down motion with your iron to press each seam instead of a back-and-forth sliding motion. Sliding the iron can distort accurately sewn seams.

• Press the seam with the fabric flat, just as it comes from the machine. Then open the fabric and press the seam to one side, following the pressing guidelines listed under each quilting technique.

• Always press a seam before you stitch a seam that crosses it.

Creating the Quilted Fashions

Log Cabin Shirt

Whenever I give seminars, I'm always flattered to see at least one participant wearing a Log Cabin shirt. Later I hear, "I made this after watching your show!"

This shirt is the perfect way to get started on quilted fashions. It's an easy project, requiring only straight-line stitching, and the finished result is very becoming. Best of all, there are no complex seams or points to match!

Modifying the Shirt Pattern

Since the Log Cabin quilt blocks are flat, the garment to which they are to be stitched must also be flat. But most patterns for sweatshirts and T-shirts have shaping in the shoulder area. Check pattern catalogs for sweatshirt or T-shirt patterns without shoulder seams; they provide the flat shoulder and neckline surfaces needed for this technique.

If you cannot find a shirt pattern without shoulder seams, modify a standard T-shirt or sweatshirt pattern following these easy instructions.

1. Work on a gridded surface, such as a rotary cutting mat. The grid markings make it easy to align the pattern so that the grain line remains straight.

2. Align the center front and center back along one of the grid markings on the cutting mat. Because these centers will be placed on a fold of the fabric when the shirt is cut out, they must form a continuous line.

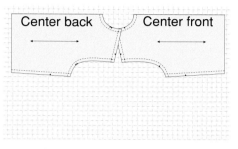

3. Overlap the front and back patterns at the neckline edge, positioning stitching line on top of stitching line as if the seam had been sewn. The pattern separates at the armhole edge, forming a V-shaped open area. Don't worry! This is exactly what should happen.

4. Position the sleeve pattern at the edge of the armhole. The sleeve will be cut all in one with the remainder of the shirt.

• Align the large dot at the center of the sleeve cap with the center of the V-opening between the front and back patterns.

• Overlap the seam allowances, placing the sleeve stitching line on top of the armhole stitching line at the sleeve cap. The sleeve grain line should be parallel to one of the grid markings on the cutting mat.

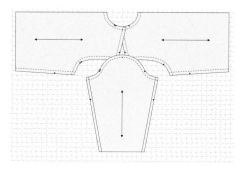

5. Place a piece of tissue paper or pattern tracing material over the pattern pieces. Extend the sleeve underarm into the side seam of the garment, forming a one-piece pattern for the shirt and sleeve.

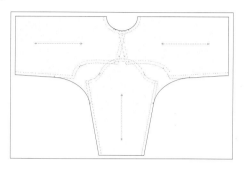

Check the length of the shoulder/sleeve seam by measuring from the base of your neck to your wrist bone. Measure the modified pattern and lengthen or shorten the pattern as needed.

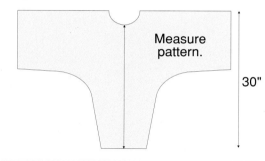

Measure pattern.

30"

Note from Nancy
Because the pattern will be placed on 60"-wide fabric, it is essential that the measurement from the center of the garment to the sleeve hemline is no more than 30". If this measurement exceeds 30", the pattern will not fit on the fabric.

6. Fold the 60"-wide fabric in half lengthwise. Place the modified pattern on the fabric, positioning both the center front and the center back along the fold. Cut out the pattern piece.

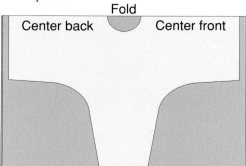

Choosing Fabrics for the Log Cabin Blocks

The key to the Log Cabin design is the contrast between the brilliant center square and the strips of dark and light fabrics. Because the shirt uses only four quilted blocks, it requires a minimum of fabric. Search your scrap box! Experiment with fabric strips until your color selection creates a pleasing arrangement. Or use this opportunity to purchase one or more fabrics to complement your stash.

1. Select three intensities of light fabrics:
   - A light light-colored fabric
   - A medium light-colored fabric
   - A dark light-colored fabric
2. Select three intensities of dark fabrics:
   - A light dark-colored fabric
   - A medium dark-colored fabric
   - A dark dark-colored fabric

Making a Sample Block

Before cutting all the strips for your Log Cabin shirt, make a sample block by arranging the fabrics on a square piece of paper. This enables you to get an idea of how the colors and fabrics will look in the finished project before you cut and sew all of the blocks. It's much easier to change fabrics at this point than to wait until all the fabrics have been cut into strips!

Note from Nancy

The logs in a traditional Log Cabin block are added in the order of two light, two dark, etc. This produces a block divided diagonally into a light and a dark triangle.

To make the sample Log Cabin block:

1. Cut a sheet of paper the size of your finished Log Cabin block. Find the center of the paper by folding it in half lengthwise and then folding again crosswise.

2. Cut a strip of each fabric 2" wide by the width of the fabric (about 45").

3. Place the fabric strips on the paper in the order that you plan to sew them.
   - Select a brilliant fabric of a strong intensity for the center of the block. Cut a 2" square of this center fabric and place it in the middle of the paper.

Timesaving Notions

Overmatching fabrics with similar values (lightness or darkness) can be a problem with quilting. The Fabric Value Filter helps me to determine the difference in value between fabrics. The fluorescent pink acrylic plastic filter actually cancels out the color and allows the light or dark value of the fabric to show. It is small and easily tucks into my purse for fabric shopping trips.

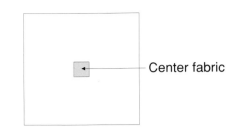

Center fabric

- Cut a 2" square of the lightest light fabric and place it to the right of the center square.
- Add a second strip of the lightest light above the two squares, working in a counterclockwise fashion, trimming the strip to the needed length. Note that the strips get longer as they go around the block.

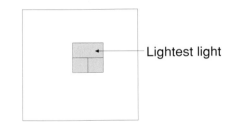

Lightest light

- Next add two strips of the lightest dark-colored fabric, always adding strips in a counterclockwise direction.

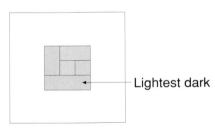

Lightest dark

- Add two medium light strips to the block; then add two medium dark strips.

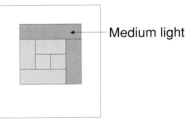

Medium light

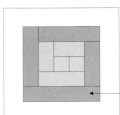

Medium dark

• Finally, add the two darkest light strips and then the two darkest dark strips.

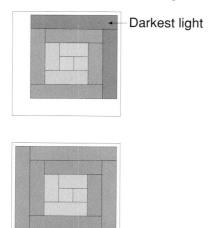

Darkest light

Darkest dark

• Analyze your design. If you don't like the effect, replace some of the strips with different fabrics. When you are satisfied with the fabrics and their arrangement, pin or tape the strips into position.

4. To use the completed sample block as a reference, number the strips, beginning with the center square as #1. Continuing in the same counterclockwise fashion that you placed the strips, label the lightest light fabric strips #2 and #3, the lightest dark fabric strips #4 and #5, and so forth.

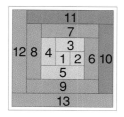

Cutting the Strips

Now that you have decided on the arrangement of the quilt strips, you are ready to cut enough strips to complete your blocks. Follow these guidelines and the cutting techniques listed on pages 32 and 33 for perfect Log Cabin strips.

1. Referring to the numbers on your sample block, cut 2"-wide strips of each 45"-wide fabric as follows:

#1: One strip for the fabric centers.
#2 and #3: One strip of the lightest light-colored fabric.
#4 and #5: One strip of the lightest dark-colored fabric.

#6 and #7: Two strips of the medium light-colored fabric.
#8 and #9: Two strips of the medium dark-colored fabric.
#10 and #11: Two strips of the darkest light-colored fabric.
#12 and #13: Two strips of the darkest dark-colored fabric.

2. Number and organize the strips on a cutting board, tray, or table. Using the numbered sample block you created earlier as a guide, place the strips in rows with #1 at the right. You're ready to sew!

Note from Nancy

I like to organize my quilt strips on a bath towel. I can roll it up and carry it safely to my sewing machine without losing any pieces. When I must stop sewing, I simply roll up the towel with the remaining pieces and tuck it into my "ready-to-sew" basket.

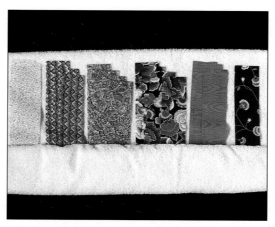

Piecing the Log Cabin Blocks

Now you are ready to piece the blocks. Use this easy, updated method to piece all four blocks at once.

1. For the center and first log, cut 10" lengths of strips #1 and #2.

2. To join strip #1 to strip #2:
• Place strip #2 right side up under the presser foot.
• With right sides together, align the cut edges of strip #1 with the edges of strip #2.
• Sew or serge the two strips together along one long edge, using a ¼" seam allowance.

Timesaving Notions

I like using Sewer's Fix-It-Tape or Pattern Pals to help number my quilt strips. You can easily write on the tape or Pattern Pals. The pressure-sensitive Pattern Pals are reusable and lift off completely without water, brushing, or other special steps.

• Press the seam allowance toward strip #2.

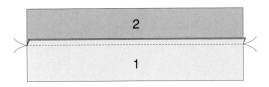

> **Note from Nancy**
> Throughout the piecing process, always press the seams away from the center square and toward the last strip added to the block.

3. Using a rotary cutter, board, and ruler, cut four 2" sections from the pieced strip to make four pieced sections. Stack the pieced sections with wrong sides up, with strip #2 at the upper edge.

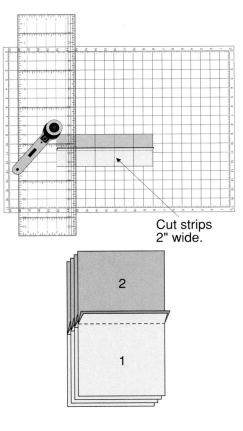

Cut strips 2" wide.

4. To join strip #3:
• Place strip #3 right side up under the presser foot.
• With right sides together, align the cut edges of one of the pieced sections with one long edge of strip #3. Strip #2 should be at the upper edge of the pieced section.

• Stitch or serge a ¼" seam, with the pressed seam allowance between strips #1 and #2 facing upward (toward strip #2).

• Butt a second of the pieced blocks to the first section. Stitch or serge. Repeat until all four pieced blocks have been stitched or serged to strip #3.

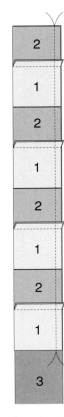

• Cut through strip #3 between the pieced sections.

• Press the seam allowances toward strip #3.

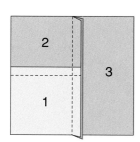

• Stack the pieced blocks wrong side up, with strip #3 at the upper edge.

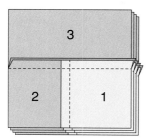

5. Join the remaining strips to the pieced block in numerical order, following the same procedure.

• Always place the new strip under the presser foot, right side up.

• Align the edges of the pieced block and the strip, placing right sides together. Always place the last joined strip at the upper edge.

• Always position the new strip perpendicular to the last strip joined to the pieced block.

• Stitch accurate ¼" seams.

• Join the four pieced blocks to the new strip with continuous stitching, butting ends of the pieced blocks together.

• Cut the blocks apart by cutting through the new strip, following the edges of the pieced block.

• Press all seam allowances away from the center.

Joining the Log Cabin Blocks

After the four Log Cabin blocks have been completed, it's time to join the blocks and place the completed block on your garment. Experiment with block placements until you find a design you like. For instance, if you join the edges of the light-colored sides of the blocks, you get a symmetrical pattern that is often called "Barn Raising."

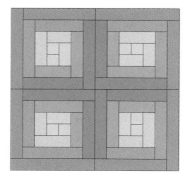

Or alternate the light and dark sides of the blocks for an asymmetrical pattern traditionally called "Fields and Furrows."

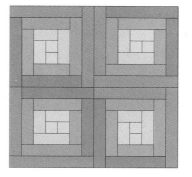

Don't be restricted to conventional designs. Move the blocks around until you find a design you like.

To join the four Log Cabin blocks:

1. With right sides together and raw edges aligned, stitch the top two blocks together along the center seam. Press the seam toward block #2.

2. Repeat, joining the bottom two blocks; press the seam toward block #3. By pressing the seams in opposite directions, bulk is reduced where the two sections are joined.

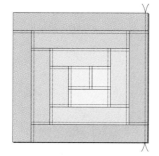

3. With right sides together and raw edges aligned, stitch the two sets of joined blocks together along the center horizontal seam. Press the seam to one side.

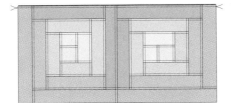

Finishing the Edges of the Joined Blocks

Finish the outer edges of the joined blocks in one of these ways:

1. Turn under ¼" along the outer edges and machine-baste.

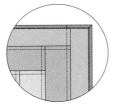

2. Add lace to the outer edges.

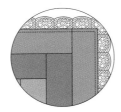

3. Bond the hem using ThreadFuse.
• Set up your serger or sewing machine using ThreadFuse in the lower looper of the serger or in the bobbin of the sewing machine.
• Serge or sew the edges with the right side up, so that the ThreadFuse is on the wrong side of the quilt blocks.
• Turn under ¼" on the outer edges and press. ThreadFuse bonds with a touch of the iron, securing the edges of the narrow hem.

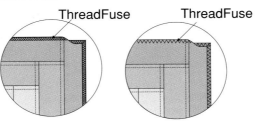

ThreadFuse   ThreadFuse

Adding the Log Cabin Blocks to the Shirt

Now you are ready to add the Log Cabin blocks to the modified T-shirt or sweatshirt you cut out earlier.

1. Mark the center front, center back, and shoulder positions of the shirt, using a washable marker or pins, or by folding the fabric and pressing lightly.

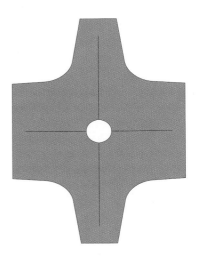

2. Mark the center of the Log Cabin blocks.

3. Position Log Cabin blocks over shirt.
• Place the corners of the Log Cabin blocks at the markings on the shirt's center front, center back, and shoulders. The center of the blocks should be centered over the shirt's neckline opening.
• Machine-stitch the blocks to the shirt, stitching along the outer edges.

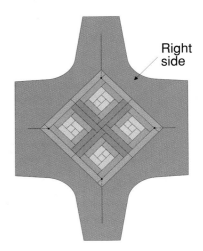

Right side

• Turn the shirt to the wrong side. Pin the block section to the shirt around the neckline opening. Stitch around the neckline.

Timesaving Notions
ThreadFuse is a polyester thread coated with a heat-activated fusible fiber. I like using this thread to bond seams or hems.

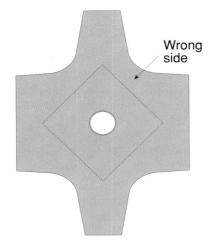

Wrong side

4. Complete the shirt.
- Stitch the shirt's side seams.

Wrong side

- Add ribbing to the neckline, waist, and wrist edges.

Note from Nancy
Now that you know the basics, you can vary the techniques to create unique shirts for yourself and others. This Log Cabin shirt features one print as the "light" side of the Log Cabin and another for the "dark" side. Experiment with different prints, solids, or setting combinations. Or go beyond the Log Cabin quilt block. Any joined quilt blocks measuring 20" to 22" square can be applied in the same manner. Use your ingenuity! The options in both fabric and design are almost limitless.

Bargello Beauties

Bargello usually refers to a needlepoint stitch that produces a zigzag pattern. This flamelike design can be easily translated into fabric, inspiring new quilting creations. Bargello quilting is a free-form type of quilting where you can definitely be a fabric artist! Here are some guidelines to get you started.

Basic Bargello
This shirt features a basic bargello design in a 12" quilted panel down the center front. Fabric strips of different colors and widths are used to create the effect.

1. Raid your fabric scrap box and select an assortment of fabrics for the bargello design. Unlike Log Cabin quilting, bargello quilting has no rules about the numbers or intensities of fabrics used for the design. Combine contrasting or coordinating colors until you are satisfied with the effect. Remember, for easier garment care, use fabrics with similar weight and fiber content.

2. Cut all fabric strips the same width. (Some common widths to consider are 2", 2½", or 3".) The *specific* width of the strips is not important, but it *is* essential that all strips are the same width so that seam intersections will match in the completed bargello piece. For easiest cutting, use rotary cutting tools and follow the cutting directions given on pages 32 and 33.

3. Arrange the strips horizontally.

• Experiment with strip placement to create a pleasing flow of color. Move the strips around until you are satisfied with the arrangement.

• Add strips until the total length equals the length required for the section or project. In the shirt pictured, the total length required is the center front length of the garment, measured from the neckline to the ribbing.

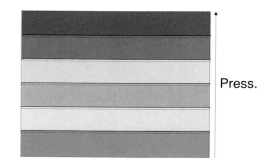

Press.

Note from Nancy

When measuring the strips, remember to subtract one-half inch from the width of each strip to allow for seam allowances when the strips are pieced. For example, if strips are cut 2½" wide, the seamed strips will be only 2" wide.

• Repeat colors and patterns until you have enough length for the project.

• Place the strips in the chosen order on a terry bath towel.

• Roll up the towel and carry the strips to the sewing area.

4. Sew or serge the strips together, using ¼" seams.

Note from Nancy

Be accurate as you stitch! All the seams must be of consistent width. The pieced section will be cut into strips of various widths and then the strips will be offset and rejoined. If seams vary in width, the intersections of the strips will not match in the finished bargello piece.

• Join additional strips until all have been seamed together and the completed piece is the desired length.

5. Press all the seam allowances in one direction. Hold the joined strips taut to avoid pressing in creases.

Note from Nancy

It saves time if you do all the pressing at once. First, join all the strips; then press all the seams in one direction.

6. With right sides together and the top and bottom strip aligned, join the strips into a tube.

• Stitch, using a ¼" seam allowance.

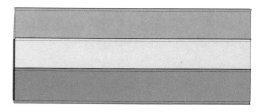

• Straighten and square one raw edge of the joined strips, using the rotary cutter, mat, and ruler.

7. Place the pieced fabric on a cutting mat and cut strips of various widths. Strips should not be narrower than ¾", but there is no maximum width. (Remember that ¼" seam allowances will be used in rejoining the strips, so the completed strips will be ½" narrower than the cut width.) There are no hard-and-fast rules. Let your imagination shape your bargello design.

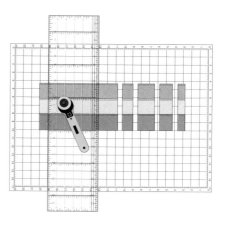

8. Position the strips to form the pattern.

• To use the darkest block as the starting point of the bargello pattern, remove the seam joining two of the strips at that position. This places the darkest block as the first block of the strip. Flatten the pieced strip.

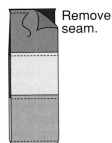

Remove seam.

• Offset the next strip, moving the top block of the first strip up or down one position by removing the seam in a different location. For example, if the block is moved down one section, the darkest block will be the second block in the second strip. Place the pieced strip next to strip #1.

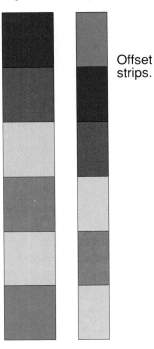

Offset strips.

• Continue placing additional pieced strips after removing the seams and moving the same colored block up or down one position each time. A "rise and fall" pattern, resembling a flame stitch, is created as more strips are added to the assembly.

• Stack the pieced strips in sequence on a terry towel. Roll up the towel and carry the towel and strips to the sewing machine or serger.

9. With right sides together and raw edges aligned, sew or serge the pieced strips together in sequence.

• Carefully match the seam allowances so that the seam intersections of adjoining strips meet. If strips are cut and seamed accurately, this should not be difficult.

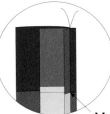

Match seams.

• Stitch or serge the seams in the same direction that the original seam allowances were pressed. This directional stitching keeps the seam allowances flat and neat, preventing tucks or bubbles from forming at seam intersections on the right side of the pieced section.

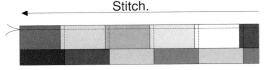

Stitch.

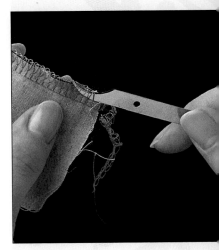

• After all strips have been joined, press all seam allowances in one direction.

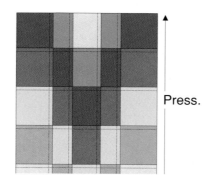

Press.

• Cut the bargello section to fit the project. The shirt shown used a 12"-wide center section of bargello with color-blocked sides.

Divided Bargello

Here's another form of bargello quilting in which the pieced bargello strips are separated by an unpieced strip of a printed fabric. Divided bargello is even easier than basic bargello, because the seam intersections do not need to match perfectly!

1. Select the fabrics.

• Choose a printed fabric as the basis for the design. Select this fabric before determining the remainder of the fabrics.

• Select several of the solid colors from the printed fabric for the pieced strips. (Don't use the printed fabric as one of the fabrics for the pieced strips—doing so interrupts the natural flow of the bargello design.)

2. Cut the bargello strips.

• Cut all the printed fabric strips the same width. Again, the *specific* width of the strips is not important—it *is* essential that all strips are the same.

For the sake of clarity, the print strips are shown a a solid color in the illustrations.

• Cut and join fabrics for the pieced strips following the same procedure as for basic bargello.

• Join the pieced fabrics into a tube. Cut the tube into strips following the same procedure as for basic bargello. These strips may be cut all the same width, or they may vary in width. (Using several strip widths and repeating the print makes it easier to establish a flow in the design.)

3. Join the bargello strips.

• Arrange the strips, alternating the pieced bargello and the printed fabric. With right sides together, stitch or serge a pieced strip to a printed strip.

• Stitch or serge another pieced strip to the remaining edge of the printed strip. Offset the fabrics up and down to produce an attractive design.

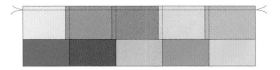

• Repeat, adding strips until the divided bargello piece is large enough for your project.

Double Bargello

For a bold and dramatic look, try another bargello alternative—double bargello. For this technique, two different bargello sections are prepared. Each section is a different combination of strip sizes, yet each shows some of the same fabrics. The strips of the two sections are alternated, producing a vibrant graphic effect. Try using solid fabrics in bold colors for the most striking result.

1. Create two bargello sections with identical finished lengths.

• Prepare one of the bargello sections, which we will call Section A, using strips cut the same width. For example, use strips in four bold colors. Join the strips as detailed for basic bargello, but *do not* join the strips into a tube. (The various colors in the strips will not be offset in the pieced section.)

Section A

• Prepare a second bargello section (Section B) using strips in various widths. Add more colors to this section, if desired. Join the strips as detailed for basic bargello. *Do not* join the strips into a tube.

Section B

Note from Nancy

For this technique, you can disregard the general guideline that all bargello strips should be cut the same width. Seam intersections will not be matched in the double bargello design, so using strips of various widths produces interesting variations.

2. Cut strips from each of the pieced sections.

• Cut all strips from Section A the same width. The example shown uses 2½" strips.

• Cut all strips from Section B a different width from Section A. The example uses 1½" strips.

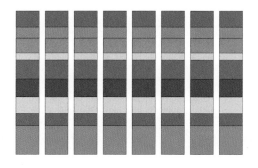

Note from Nancy

Use scraps to test the effect of your double bargello design. It's the best way to determine whether you will like the finished result. When you are satisfied with the arrangement, cut all of the strips for your project.

3. With right sides together and raw edges aligned, alternating strips A and B, stitch or serge the strips, using a ¼" seam allowance. The strips are *not* offset; they are in the same position each time, with strips A and B alternating. Continue alternating the strips until the completed pieced section is the desired width.

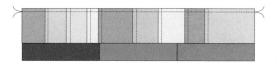

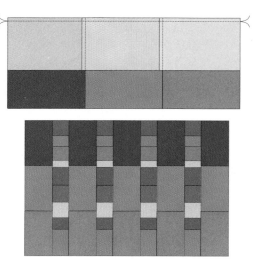

4. Add the pieced section to the completed garment or project.

Pseudo Bargello

This is the easiest of all bargello options! The finished design looks as if you carefully matched intersections of several different fabrics, but the "strips" are actually sections of a striped fabric. Consider adding pseudo bargello to one or both sleeves, a pocket, or just the back of your garment. The olive jacket shown here uses a pseudo bargello design only on the right half of the front.

1. Select a striped fabric with a dominant design. Distinctive colors or designs in the stripes will result in a more striking bargello piece.

2. Cut strips of various widths from the fabric, cutting perpendicular to the stripes.

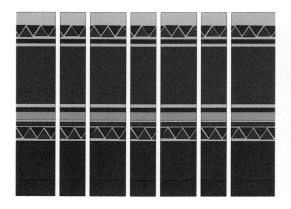

3. Arrange the cut strips, staggering the position of the stripes to create the pseudo bargello effect.

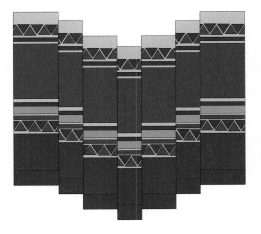

4. With right sides together and raw edges aligned, stitch or serge the strips together along the long vertical edges.

5. Square off any uneven top and bottom edges and join the section to the garment.

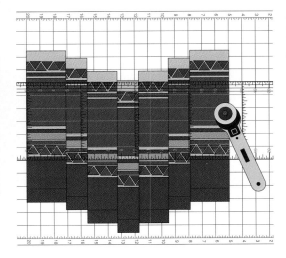

Seminole Accents

Seminole Indians were the first artisans to embellish their clothing with quilted geometric shapes cut and pieced from vivid fabrics. We will borrow the Seminole designs but use contemporary strip-piecing techniques to update this decorative accent from the southeastern United States.

Let's begin this section with the basics to give you a foundation in Seminole piecing. Then let your imagination flow! Experiment with combining prints, solids, and textures. Add Seminole accents to a skirt border, a shirt yoke, jacket, vest, towel, tote bag, shower curtain, place mat, napkin, table runner, tablecloth, pillow, and more. It's a sewing accent that will inspire creativity!

Basic Three-Strip Seminole Piecing

Use strip-quilting methods to simplify Seminole piecing.

1. Select three coordinating or contrasting fabrics. They may be solids, small prints, or a combination of both. If the fabrics are lightweight, fuse interfacing to the wrong side of the fabric to aid in handling.

2. Cut three crosswise fabric strips (selvage to selvage) the same width (1" to 3" wide). For this project, the strips were cut 1½" wide.

3. Stack the strips, with one color to each pile. Position the stacks in the order in which they will be sewn. Place the dominant color, or the one you wish to emphasize, in the center of the three stacks.

4. Sew or serge the strips together, using ¼" seams.

• Take a strip from each of the first two piles. With right sides together and raw edges aligned, stitch together along one long edge.

Note from Nancy
Stitching each seam allowance exactly the same width is a must with Seminole piecing so that the seams will match.

• If more than one length of each color is needed to produce enough fabric for the Seminole section, you can save time by joining strips with continuous or chain piecing.

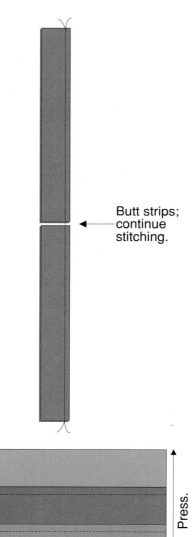

Butt strips; continue stitching.

Press.

• With right sides together, join the third color strip to the remaining long raw edge of the center strip. Stitch together with

a ¼" seam. Using the continuous piecing technique, repeat to join the remaining strips. Cut the thread chains between the strips and press the seams in one direction.

5. Cut the joined strips into pieces the same width as the original width of the individual strips. (For this project, cut the strips into 1½" pieces.) If you are Seminole-piecing a large area that requires many pieces, cut several layers at once by carefully stacking the strips and using rotary cutting tools.

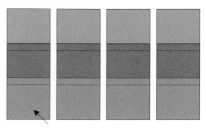

Cut pieces 1½" wide.

6. Join the fabric pieces.
• Stack the fabric pieces in two piles, right sides up, with the same color at the top of each strip.
• Take one piece from each pile and place right sides together, aligning long raw edges.
• Offset the pieces by moving one piece down the width of one strip.

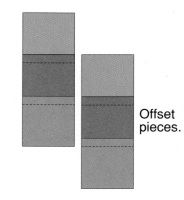

Offset pieces.

• Serge or sew the pieces together, using a ¼" seam.

Note from Nancy
The key to making attractive Seminole piecing is accurately matching the seam intersections. Place a pin at the crucial intersection where the two fabrics meet. One pin per seam is all that's needed.

• After joining one set of strips, continue by chain piecing the remaining sets of strips. (Refer to the techniques on page 34 for help with chain piecing.)

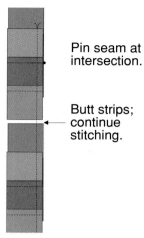

Pin seam at intersection.

Butt strips; continue stitching.

• Continue joining the remaining pieces in the same manner.

• Cut the strips apart and press the seams in one direction.

7. Sew the pairs together.

• Divide the pairs into two stacks, keeping the colors in the same order.

• Take one pair from each stack, place right sides together, and offset the pieces by moving one pair down the width of one strip. Match the pieces exactly at the seam intersections and stitch, using a ¼" seam.

• Join the next set of pairs to the first set, following the same procedures, and stitch. Continue until all the pairs are joined.

• Cut the strips apart and press the seams in one direction.

8. Continue in the same manner until all the sections are pieced and the strip is the desired width.

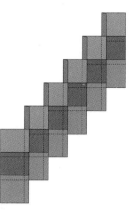

9. Use the strip as desired to embellish a garment or project. To add a border to the Seminole strip, see page 51.

Diamond Seminole Piecing

Contrasting fabrics can be used to create a small accent on a garment like this camisole. Such a quilting embellishment adds charm without being overwhelming.

1. Cut three to five strips of different colored fabrics, all measuring the same width. (For the camisole, the strips were cut 1½" wide.) An uneven number of strips is needed for the diamond design.

• With right sides together and raw edges aligned, stitch the strips together along the long edges, using ¼" seams.

• Press the seam allowances in one direction.

2. To achieve a diamond effect, the Seminole pieces must be cut at a 45° angle. To cut this angle:

• Measure the width of the joined strips.

• Measure an identical distance along the length of the pieced strip and mark. This identifies a square section of fabric.

• Place a ruler from corner to corner of the square. Cut along this line, using a rotary cutter or shears, to make a 45° angle.

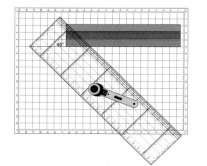

Timesaving Notions
I like using my quilting ruler, which includes a marked 45° angle, for precise cutting. Simply position the line indicating the 45° angle along the lower edge of the fabric and use a rotary cutter and cutting mat to cut accurate angles every time.

• Cut all strips the same width, measuring from the diagonal edge. (The strips for the camisole were cut 1½" wide.) If the design requires a lot of Seminole strips, cut two layers at the same time. Stack the layers face down on the cutting mat and cut.

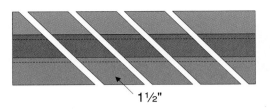

1½"

• Make two stacks of the cut strips as you did for the basic Seminole piecing.

3. To join the strips:

• Place two strips with right sides together, offsetting the strips by one fabric width. To assure precise matching, turn the fabric strips to the wrong side. Measure ¼" from the edge of the strips to find the seam line and mark it with a washable marker.

• Poke a pin through the top strip at the mark. Come out at the mark on the lower strip and pin. Stitch the edges together.

Pin seam intersection.

• Stitch the remaining pairs together, using the continuous piecing technique described on page 34. Cut the thread chains between the pairs.

• Join the pairs together and continue until all the strips are joined into a strip with a diamond effect.

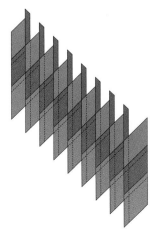

Seminole Stripes

Striped fabrics are naturals for Seminole accents—they enable you to bypass many of the basic preliminary cutting and stitching steps. Cut the striped fabric on the bias, alternate the stripe direction, and you have a simple "Seminole" stripe accent with a minimum amount of sewing.

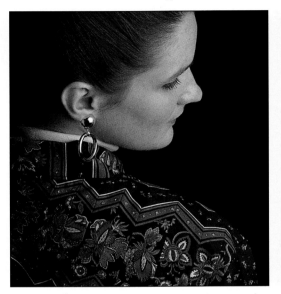

1. Select a striped fabric. Although stripes of any width may be used, narrow stripes generally create a more pleasing effect than wider stripes. Stripes may be even or uneven in width.

2. Cut a strip of fabric the width of the desired Seminole accent. Cut the strip on the crosswise grain so that the stripes run the length of the strip.

3. Fold the strip in half crosswise (short ends meeting), with right sides together and stripes matching. If fabric strips are short, use two pieces with identical stripes, placing right sides together.

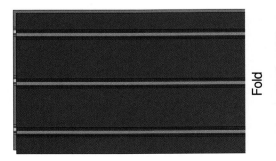

Fold

4. Cut the folded strip at a 45° angle, cutting through both layers of fabric to form striped pairs.

- Measure the width of the strip. Then measure and mark an identical distance on the length of the strip.
- Place a ruler from corner to corner of the marked square and cut.

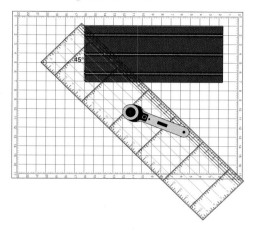

- Cut strips through both layers of fabric to create pairs of striped fabric. The strips need not be all of the same width—you can vary the widths for an interesting effect. The crucial factor is that all pieces are cut at a 45° angle and in pairs.

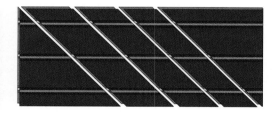

5. With right sides together, and making sure that the stripes match exactly, join one pair of strips, using a ¼" seam.

6. Butt another pair to the first pair and continue stitching. Repeat until all the pairs have been joined.

7. Clip threads between the pairs, press the seams open, and continue with the garment as in basic three-strip Seminole piecing.

Seminole Finishing Techniques
Straightening the Ends of the Bands

Joined Seminole pattern bands will have angles at their ends. This simple technique creates more usable area by making the ends straight.

1. At one intersection, place a ruler on the straight of the grain through the centers of the squares. Cut through the intersection.

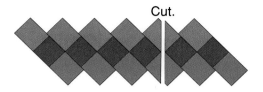

Cut.

2. With right sides together, join the two angled ends, offsetting one section and matching the seam intersections. This creates a totally usable strip of fabric with right-angled ends.

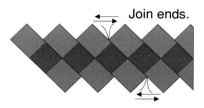

Join ends.

Straightening the Edges of the Seminole Strip

1. Place the Seminole piece right side down on the cutting board with the central pattern parallel to one of the horizontal lines.

2. Use a ruler and marking pen or pencil to mark a stitching line on the wrong side of the top and bottom edges of the Seminole piece. The lines will run through the intersections of the offset seams.

3. Add a ¼" seam allowance and draw the cutting line.

Adding Borders to the Seminole Strip

1. Cut two border strips, 1½" to 2" wide. With right sides together, join the strips to each lengthwise edge of the Seminole piece.

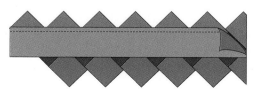

2. Stitch a ¼" seam, following the marked stitching line, on the Seminole piece. Trim off the points.

3. Press under a ¼" seam allowance along the unfinished edge of each border. Topstitch the Seminole accent to a garment or project.

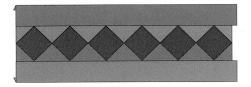

Serger Seminole Piecing

Attention, all serger owners! Here's a perfect way to combine your favorite decorative threads and the basic overlock stitch to create Seminole pieces. It's a unique combination of threads, stitches, and techniques that gives another dimension to fashion quilting.

This technique parallels the basic three-strip Seminole piecing instructions for conventional sewing machines detailed on pages 47 through 49. You may wish to review that technique prior to beginning the serger version.

1. Set up the serger for a 3-thread overlock stitch. Use an all-purpose thread in the needle and decorative threads in the upper and lower loopers. Before you begin, test the stitch length, stitch width, and thread tensions on scraps of fabric to assure smooth serging.

2. Cut the fabric strips as detailed for basic three-strip Seminole piecing. For this project, the strips were cut 2" wide.

3. With wrong sides together, serge the strips. Press the seams in one direction.

Press.

4. To finish all the raw edges, serge the ends and edges of the strips that are not seamed.

5. Cut the strips into pieces measuring the initial width of the strip. (For this project, cut the strips into pieces measuring 2" wide.) Stack the pieces in two piles, with right sides up and with the same color at the top of each strip.

6. Take one piece from each pile and place them with right sides together. Offset the pieces by moving one piece down the width of one strip.

7. Serge the pieces together along one long edge, serging the entire length of the seam, including the single layers of the seam.

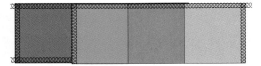

> ### Note from Nancy
> At the point where two decorative serged seams intersect, I commonly have a "bubble" of thread in the seam caused by the double layers of thread. To avoid this dilemma, I like to serge the intersecting seam with right sides together, hiding any potential serging blemish.

8. Continue serging pieces together until the desired length of the serger band is created. (See page 51, "Straightening the Ends of the Bands," to complete the piecing technique.)

9. Use a conventional sewing machine to topstitch the completed serged sections to the garment or project.

Blooming Fabric

Add dimension to your next quilted garment by creating a "blooming" fabric! Stack six layers of fabric, grid and stitch in one-inch increments, and cut some of the layers to create the blooms. Then run your finished garment through several cycles of the washer and dryer to encourage the fabric petals to come out in their full glory! What a lively way to add texture, color, and dimension to a jacket, vest, or sweatshirt!

Choosing Fabric for the Vest

To create a blooming effect like the one on the featured vest, use six layers of fabric. Choose compatible weights of 100% cotton fabrics (wash and dry the fabric before cutting).

The outer layer and lining can be the same color, with the middle layers in different colors. Black, white, navy, and yellow are choices that will help define and separate the middle layers.

Choosing and Modifying the Pattern

Because the vest is made from six layers of fabric, choose a pattern that has no darts and a minimum number of seams.

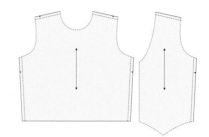

To modify the pattern:

1. Trim the seam allowances from the neckline, armholes, and hemline so that only the shoulder and side seams retain the seam allowances. These pattern pieces will be used to cut the outer layer and the lining.

2. Make a pattern for the middle layers by placing waxed paper over the modified pattern pieces. Trace the finished size of the pattern, eliminating all of the seam allowances.

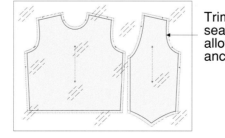

Trim seam allowances.

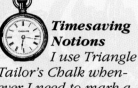

Cutting the Pieces for the Vest

1. Using the modified front and back pattern pieces, cut out the outer fabric and lining.

2. Using the waxed paper front and back pattern pieces, cut out the four middle layers of fabric.

> ### Note from Nancy
> I use my rotary cutter and mat to cut all four middle layers at the same time. I stack the fabric layers in the desired order, place the waxed paper pattern on top, and cut. Cutting is accomplished quickly, and I know that all layers are identical.

Marking the Grid

1. With right sides together, stitch the shoulder seams of the outer fabric pieces, joining the fronts to the back. Press the seams open. Trim the seam allowances to ¼".

2. On the right sides, mark the outer fabric into 1" grids, using a ruler and tailor's chalk.

- Place the fabric right side up on a flat surface, opening out the pieces.
- Mark the vertical lines on the back, beginning at the center and working out to the side seams.

- If the fabric will be blooming in the area of the shoulder seams, make certain that the grids meet at the seam. Pivot the ruler and continue to mark vertical lines on the vest front, making sure that the lines are parallel with the center front line.

> ### Note from Nancy
> This attention to detail will produce an appealing garment and will make it easier to align the seams when you stitch the lines later.

- Mark the horizontal lines on the back, starting at the hemline and working up to the shoulder seams. Repeat for the front.

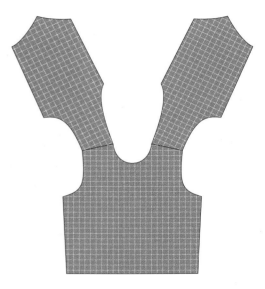

> ### Note from Nancy
> On most solid fabrics, you can save time by gridding only one vest front. Accurately align both fronts with right sides together and press with your hands. Presto! The chalk marks will transfer to the unmarked side.

Joining the Outer and Middle Fabrics

1. Place the outer fabric vest on a flat surface with the wrong side up.

2. Place the four middle layers for the back on the wrong side of the outer fabric back. Butt the cut shoulder edges of the middle layers to the stitched shoulder seam of the outer fabric and align the cut edges of all layers at the neckline and armholes. Pin all layers together at the shoulder seams and at the outer edges. Repeat for garment front.

Note from Nancy

The cut edges of the middle layers must meet exactly at the shoulder seams, with no space or overlapping. This will assure a well-fitted vest, with no gaps at the shoulder seams.

3. Using a zigzag stitch, baste the shoulder seams of the middle layers to the shoulder seams of the outer fabric. The zigzag stitch must catch both front and back stacks of fabric in order to anchor the middle layers to the shoulder seams of the outer fabric.

Zigzag

4. Zigzag the layers together along the raw edges of the hemline, neckline, and armholes.

5. Using a straight stitch and a long stitch length, machine-baste the layers together to prevent shifting during quilting.

• From each shoulder, stitch along a vertical grid line to the bottom edge of the back. Repeat from each shoulder to the bottom edge of the front.

• On the back, stitch one horizontal row along a grid line below the armholes and a second horizontal row 6" to 8" above the hemline. Repeat for the front pieces.

Precutting the Blooms

1. Place the vest on a rotary cutting mat, with the outer layer on top. Position the ruler diagonally across the 1" chalk grids. Use the rotary cutter to cut a ¾" diagonal slit in each grid that should "bloom."

2. Repeat for the front sections of the garment.

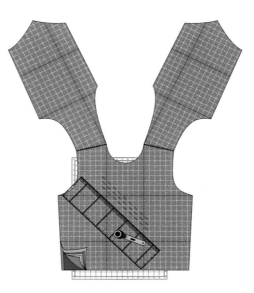

Adding the Lining

1. Place the garment on a flat surface, with the outer layer down and the middle layers up. Place the lining on the garment, with the right side up, and pin it in place.

2. Turn the garment to the right side. Machine-baste the lining to the garment, stitching in-the-ditch at the shoulder seams from the right side, securing all the layers.

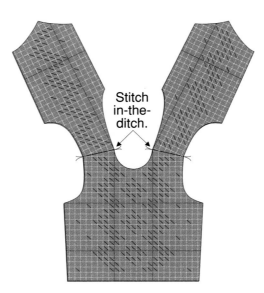

Stitch in-the-ditch.

Timesaving Notions

The Bias Tape Maker quickly and neatly folds under the raw edges of bias strips, easing the task of making yards of bias tape. Slip the bias strip wrong side up through the wide end of the tape maker, slide the fabric through the funnel-shaped tube, and press the folded tape at the narrower point. The lengthwise raw edges automatically fold to the center.

The size of the tape maker indicates the width of the bias strip after the raw edges are pressed to the center. The 1" size is best suited for garment construction.

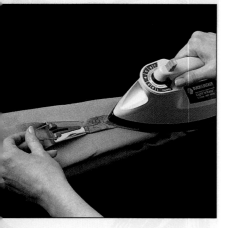

Quilting the Vest

1. To set up the sewing machine:
• Insert a size 90 (14) needle in the machine.
• Set the machine for a straight stitch, with the stitch length at 10 stitches per inch.

2. To stitch the vertical grid lines:
• Begin by stitching the vertical line at the center back. Next, stitch one of the vertical lines nearest the center and continue working outward to the side seam.
• Alternate the stitching direction with each line. Starting at the neckline, stitch to the lower edge. On the next line, stitch from the lower edge to the neckline. Stitch the third line from the neck to the bottom edge.

• Stitch the grid lines that cross the shoulder seams in one continuous line, pivoting at the shoulder seam.

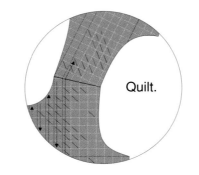

Quilt.

• Repeat to complete the remaining vertical grid lines.

3. In the same manner, stitch the horizontal grid lines, alternating stitching directions.

4. Remove the basting stitches in the grid area.

5. Stitch the side seams.

Finishing the Blooms

1. To cut each bloom:
• Insert the point of an embroidery scissors into the diagonal cut you made earlier with the rotary cutter.

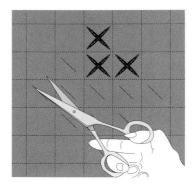

• Cut from the center to each corner, being careful not to cut the lining or the quilt stitching.

> ### Note from Nancy
> For variation, you may choose to cut only three of the four corners to achieve a partial bloom effect. This variation can be combined with squares that are cut to all four corners.

Partial bloom

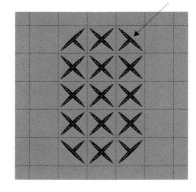

2. Remove the basting stitches (both the zigzag stitching and the in-the-ditch stitching) at the shoulder seams.

Finishing the Vest

Give the vest a slimmer look by trimming the outer edges with bias tape the same color as the vest.

1. To cut the bias strips from the outer fabric:

• Square the fabric using a rotary cutter, quilting ruler, and mat (see pages 32 and 33).

• Align the 45° mark on the ruler with one cut edge of the fabric. Cut the fabric, guiding the rotary cutter along the ruler.

• Advance the ruler so that the 2" mark aligns with the fabric's cut edge. Cut numerous 2"-wide strips.

2. You will need approximately four yards of bias tape for the binding. (The yardage needed may vary with the size of the garment.) After cutting, the short ends of each bias strip will lie at a 45° angle to the long edges.

To join the strips:

• Place the short ends of two strips with right sides together, offsetting the ends by ¼". Stitch, using a ¼" seam; press the seam open and trim off the triangular ends.

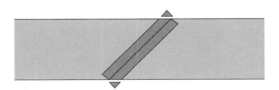

• Repeat until all bias strips are joined.

3. With wrong sides together, fold the joined bias strip in half lengthwise; press lightly, creating a press mark. Open the strip; fold the raw edges toward the center fold and press. Or use a Bias Tape Maker to simplify the pressing process.

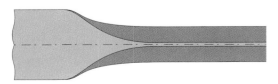

4. Preshape the bias strips to match the curves of the garment edge. Using a steam iron, lightly press the bias tape to conform to the shape of the garment.

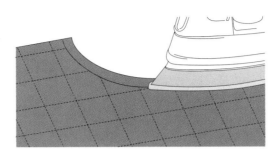

5. Apply the bias tape to the edges of the armholes and to the neckline, center front edges, and hemline.

To apply the bias tape:

• Set the sewing machine for a basting stitch. If desired, use ThreadFuse in the bobbin and all-purpose thread for the needle.

• Unfold one side of the bias strip. Turn under a ¼" hem along the narrow end of the tape; finger-press.

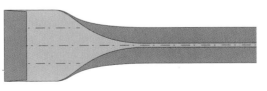

• With right sides together, align the long raw edge of the bias tape with the raw edge of the garment. Place the short edge of the bias tape at the fold at one of the garment's side seams.

• Stitch around the vest in one long seam, following the fold line of the tape for a perfect ¼" seam. At the end, overlap the bias tape slightly beyond the initial fold.

Timesaving Notions

ThreadFuse is the ideal way to apply bias tape accurately, eliminating the use of pins. Begin by loading ThreadFuse in the bobbin, using your regular thread for the needle. Stitch the bias tape to the garment with the bias tape on top so that the ThreadFuse will be stitched onto the wrong side of the garment. Fold the bias tape over the seam allowance and steam-press the tape to the back side of the fabric. Replace the ThreadFuse in the bobbin with regular thread and edgestitch the bias tape in place.

Timesaving Notions *Wonder-Under Transfer Fusing Web by Pellon is a specially designed heat-sensitive adhesive material that turns any fabric into a fusible fabric. It has a smooth paper side on which you can easily trace a design. The reverse rough side contains a bonding material that fuses the design to another fabric. It's quick, easy, and virtually foolproof.*

Wonder-Under

• Trim the excess bias tape. Stitch to secure the remaining cut edge of bias tape.

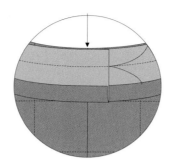

• Wrap the bias tape over the edge to the inside, covering the stitching with the remaining folded edge.
• If you used ThreadFuse in the bobbin, press the bias tape in place.
• Edgestitch the bias tape in place, stitching through all the layers.

Edgestitch.

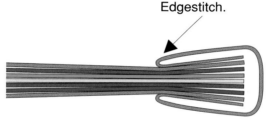

• Repeat to finish the edges of the armholes.
6. Wash and dry the garment to see it bloom!

Fuse-and-Stitch Patchwork

Quilting patterns are so versatile! Although most quilt designs are stitched or serged together, many patterns can be converted to this simple "fuse and stitch" technique. The fabrics are cut and fused to a base fabric. Then laces and ribbons are placed over the raw edges and stitched or glued in place. What a quick way to create gifts or art for the walls of your home!

1. Select a simple quilt design or pattern.
2. Choose a base fabric and an assortment of coordinating fabrics, ribbons, and laces.
3. To cut and fuse the quilt design:
• Trace the sections of the design, without seam allowances, onto the paper side of a paper-backed fusible web like Wonder-Under. (In the completed project, the raw edges of the fabrics will be covered with ribbons and laces, so seam allowances are not needed.) Note that when the design has a specific orientation, you must draw the mirror image on the paper side so that the correct alignment will appear on the right side of the project.
• Cut around each penciled section, leaving a narrow margin of Wonder-Under beyond the actual cutting line.
• Place the rough side of each Wonder-Under section against the wrong side of the fabric and press.

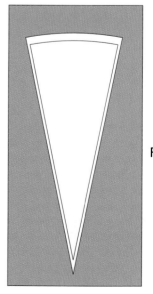

Fuse.

• Cut out each design, following the traced pattern.

• Peel the paper backing from the Wonder-Under.

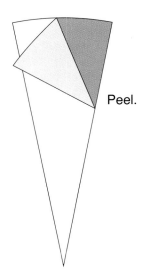

Peel.

• Position the fabric pieces backed with Wonder-Under on the base fabric, with the fusible side down. Cover with a damp cloth and fuse.

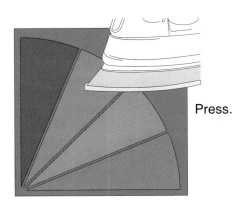

Press.

4. Cut pieces of ribbon or lace to fit along each of the raw edges of the fused fabrics. To prevent the cut ends of the ribbon or lace from raveling, overlap the ends with another section of ribbon or lace. Glue-baste or pin the laces and ribbons in place.

5. Thread the sewing machine with monofilament thread or matching all-purpose sewing machine thread. Stitch the ribbons and laces to the fabric background or glue them in place with fabric glue.

6. If desired, add lace around the outer edges of the patchwork shapes. Lace shapes easily and conforms to curved outlines more readily than ribbon.

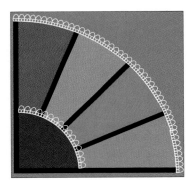

Timesaving Notions
An Appliqué Pressing Sheet is a valuable notion to use when bonding a fusible web to fabric to protect your iron and ironing board cover from the fusible resins. To use it, fold the pressing sheet in half, insert the fusible web and fabric between the two layers, and press.

Timesaving Notions
This can be a totally no-sew project! Instead of stitching the trims in place, use No-Sew Adhesive to apply decorative trims. It remains flexible, dries clear, and prevents bleed-through.

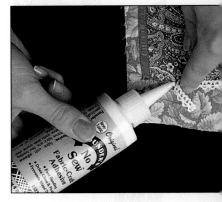

Luxurious

LINGERIE

Lingerie. The word brings to mind a picture of delicate, feminine clothing: slips, camisoles, and teddies. In this chapter, I'd like to share some of my favorite ideas for creating lingerie. Choose your favorite fabrics—silky woven fabrics for luxurious lingerie or classic knits for comfortable and easy-care garments. The sewing techniques are equally as varied—from streamlined to creative.

Sewing lingerie is fun! Let's get started.

Assembling the Elements

Choosing the Right Fabric

Woven Fabrics

Woven lingerie fabrics have luster and sheen, which add elegance to lingerie. Consider using silk, polyester, or rayon in broadcloth, charmeuse, jacquard, crepe de chine, or crepe-back satin for your next lingerie project. Cotton or cotton-blend batiste is another consideration for lingerie with a nostalgic or heirloom look. If easy care is an important feature for you, check the fiber content and care instructions at the end of the bolt before purchasing the fabric.

Knit Fabrics

Tricot (pronounced tree-ko) is the most popular knit fabric used for sewing lingerie.

Made of nylon, lingerie tricot is available in two weights. The basic weight is used for slips, camisoles, nightgowns, and panties. The sheer weight is used for overlays on camisoles and peignoirs.

Items of lingerie made from tricot fabrics with a special antistatic finish are less likely to cling to clothing than those made from traditional nylon fabrics. Tricot has 25% to 50% stretch in the crosswise direction and is available in widths ranging from 54" to 108". To identify the right side of a piece of tricot, pull the fabric on the crosswise grain. The fabric will curl or roll to the right side.

> ### Note from Nancy
> Once I have determined the right side of the tricot, I like to mark the wrong side of the fabric to avoid confusion later. After I have cut out all the fabric pieces, I simply mark the wrong side of the fabric with transparent tape or a washable marking pen.

Jerseys are single-knit fabrics made of cotton or cotton blends.

Pointelles are single knits with open areas resembling lace; the open areas are created by a pattern knit directly into the fabric.

Allover stretch lace is used to make foundation garments that help achieve the slimmer silhouette so popular today.

Cotton/spandex jersey (stretch jersey) fabric is great for exercise apparel. You'll find it used in ready-to-wear clothing such as sport bras and activewear.

Exploring Elastics and Laces

Many types of elastics and laces are available for sewing lingerie. When you choose different laces and trims to be used in the same garment, check the labels to be sure the fiber content and care instructions are similar.

Elastics

Traditional lingerie elastic is a soft elastic available in widths of ¼" and ½", usually with one scalloped or picot-trimmed edge and one straight edge. The narrower elastic is used for leg openings and the wider for waistline openings.

Stretch lace combines the best of two worlds: It's comfortable to wear because of its stretch, and it adds an attractive accent to a garment. Used for waistline or leg openings, stretch lace is available in widths of up to 4" and in a wide assortment of colors. This soft, decorative lace duplicates the look of expensive ready-to-wear lingerie at a fraction of the cost.

Sheer elastic is soft and lightweight, yet it has a tremendous amount of stretch and recovery. It is available in both black and white in a width of 1½". Sheer elastic has a shimmer or sheen and is often used for exercise clothing or activewear.

Clear elastic is used most often on activewear and swimwear. This lightweight, 100% polyurethane elastic has a tremendous amount of resilience. It stretches up to three times its length, yet retracts to its original size—an important feature for clothing designed for vigorous activity.

Laces

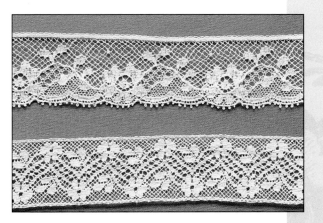

Lace for lingerie may be purchased in many colors and in widths ranging from ¼" to 2". Laces may be made entirely of nylon, polyester, or cotton, or from a blend of those fibers.

Insertion lace has two straight finished edges. It can be inserted between two pieces of fabric or between other laces and trims.

Edging laces have one straight edge and one scalloped edge. Use edging lace to finish the edges of hems and necklines.

Specialty Sewing Notions

Sewing notions can help you complete your lingerie sewing in a shorter period of time and obtain more professional results. Each specialty notion is designed to streamline your sewing.

Pattern weights can be used to "pin" the pattern to the fabric without using traditional pins, which can leave lasting holes in delicate lingerie fabrics. Weights are available in various shapes and sizes. If you use pattern weights with tacks on one side, you must invert them, placing the smooth side against the fabric so that the tacks do not snag the delicate fabric.

sheer fabrics. The slightly blunted points and the ultrafine serrated edges of the microserrated shears grip slippery fabrics without snagging as they cut, allowing precise control. The lightweight shears weigh only two ounces, yet they cut sheer fabrics with very little effort.

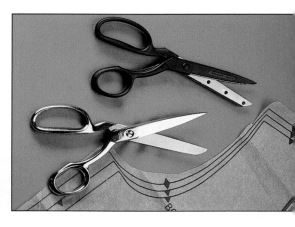

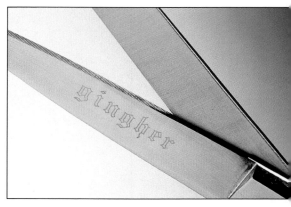

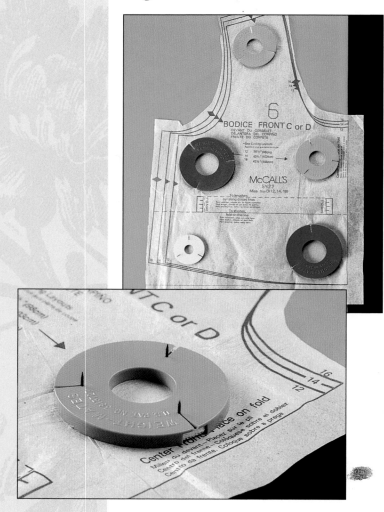

Rotary cutting tools are wonderful for cutting slippery lingerie fabrics. The small rotary cutter cuts easily around curves, producing a smooth edge.

Lightweight shears and microserrated shears cut silk and silk-like lingerie fabrics with ease, making them perfect choices for cutting out pattern pieces from slippery or

An **appliqué scissors** makes it easy to clip the fabric from behind laces or elastics without accidentally cutting the trim. (The same result can be obtained with a conventional scissors or shears—bevel the shears by holding the blades at a slant when you trim to avoid cutting the lace or elastic.)

A **sharpening stone** can restore the original sharpness to the blades of almost any knife-edge scissors or shears in very little time. Lingerie fabrics, especially nylon and other synthetic fabrics, rapidly dull the blades of shears and scissors just as they dull sewing machine needles. You'll be amazed at the difference a sharpening stone makes.

Sewer's Fix-It Tape allows you to precisely position trims as you construct a garment. It is specifically designed to remove easily and to leave no sticky residue on fabric.

Fabric glue, available in easy-to-handle sticks, is nontoxic and odorless; it easily washes out of the fabric when the project is completed. A tiny dab of glue is all you need to hold trims in place before you stitch. Less is best!

Insta-Pin is a "glue stick in a bottle." It bonds the lace to the fabric as you sew, yet easily washes out when you're finished. And it won't gum up machine needles. Again, a little of this product goes a long way!

Silk pins are extra-sharp pins that are shorter and much thinner than traditional pins. Silk pins pass through fine fabrics more readily, reducing the possibility of puckering. Because these pins must be strong despite their small diameter, they are made of nonstainless steel. Silk pins may rust if stored in a damp area.

Stretch or ballpoint needles, size 75 European (11 American), are best when sewing knit fabrics. The needles have slightly rounded tips that pass between the fibers rather than piercing them. This helps prevent skipped stitches.

Universal point needles, size 70 European (10 American), are recommended for woven fabrics. Using these needles when you work on fine lingerie fabrics will help reduce the likelihood of getting snags, pulls, or unsightly holes in your fabric.

> ### Note from Nancy
> *Before starting each lingerie project, insert a new sewing machine needle. Lingerie fabrics dull needles very quickly, and a new needle improves the quality of the stitch and helps prevent skipped stitches.*

Washable marking pens or pencils are used to transfer pattern details or to mark the position of laces and trims on the fabric. After the markings are no longer needed, they can be easily removed with a dab of water.

Lingerie/Bobbin Thread is a soft and supple braided nylon thread that stretches slightly as you sew knits. The thread is almost transparent and blends with the fabric. When sewing woven fabrics, use a thread with a fiber content similar to that of the fabric.

Texturized nylon thread, such as Metroflock Woolly Stretch Nylon, is recommended for serging knits. This texturized thread gives the serged seam a degree of stretch comparable to that of the fabric, reducing the possibility that the stitches will pop as the garment is worn.

Successful Techniques for Beautiful Lingerie

Selecting and Modifying the Pattern

Changing the Grain Line

Lingerie garments must be able to stretch with the body. For this reason, most lingerie patterns are designed for knit fabrics with the stretch of the fabric (the crosswise grain) going around the body.

After a simple pattern change, garments such as slips, panties, and camisoles, intended to be made from knits, can be made from woven fabrics as well. Simply place the pattern pieces on the bias to provide the necessary degree of stretch. Here's how to change the pattern grain line.

1. If the pattern piece is designed to be cut on the fold, make a complete pattern piece.

• Trace and cut out half the pattern, cutting to the fold line.

• Flip the pattern over, align the fold lines on the original and traced pattern pieces, and cut out the remaining half of the pattern.

• Transfer the original grain line to the completed pattern piece.

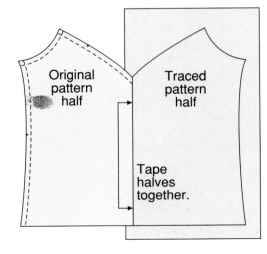

2. Modify the grain line from straight grain to bias.

- Mark a line at right angles to the original grain line.

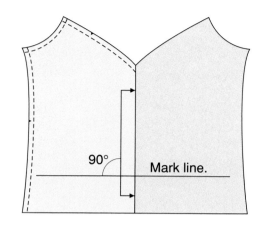

90°   Mark line.

- Fold the pattern, aligning the original grain line with the perpendicular line; press flat with your fingers.
- Mark along the crease. This new marked line, at a 45° angle to the original grain line, is on the true bias.

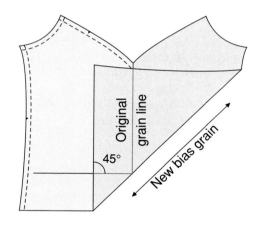

Original grain line

45°

New bias grain

3. Cut out the modified pattern from a single thickness of fabric.

Note from Nancy

Changing the pattern grain line may increase the amount of fabric required for the pattern. Try a practice layout before you pin and cut out garment pieces. Although you may need slightly more yardage than the pattern indicates, I think that you will be pleased with the drape of the fabric and with the comfort of the finished garment.

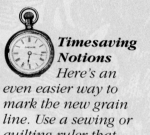

Timesaving Notions

Here's an even easier way to mark the new grain line. Use a sewing or quilting ruler that includes a marked 45° angle (Salem, O'lipfa, or Omnigrid rulers all work well). Position the ruler's 45° angle along the original pattern grain line. Trace along one of the ruler's straight outer edges, and you'll have a perfect bias grain line.

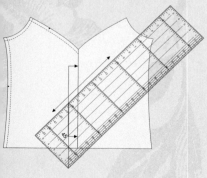

Experimenting with Seams

You have many stitching options when seaming lingerie. In addition to the usual straightstitched or zigzagged seam available on a conventional sewing machine, try one of these seaming options. You'll get great results!

Speedy French Seams

A French seam is the perfect choice for joining garments made of delicate lingerie fabrics. With two rows of straightstitching and a little pressing, the raw edges of the fabric are encased attractively and neatly.

To join two garment pieces with a French seam:

1. With *wrong* sides together and raw edges aligned, straightstitch ⅜" from the cut edges.

2. Using a rotary cutter and cutting mat, trim the seam allowance to just slightly less than ¼".

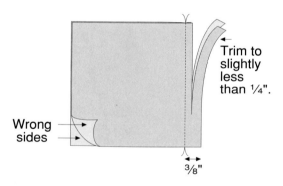

Trim to slightly less than ¼".

Wrong sides

⅜"

3. Press the joined edges flat and then press the seam open. This makes it easier to fold the seam allowance along the first stitching line in preparation for the second row of machine stitching.

4. Refold the seam allowance so that the *right* sides of the fabric are together, positioning the first stitching line at the fold. Stitch ¼" from the fold, encasing the cut edges to complete the French seam.

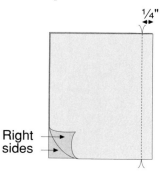

¼"

Right sides

Double Zigzag Seam

This basic sewing machine seam is appropriate for both knit and woven fabrics. For knits, two rows of side-by-side zigzag stitches provide the stretch needed for the garment's durability and comfort. For woven fabrics, which require less stretch, one row of straightstitching alongside a row of zigzag stitching is the simplest seam.

To produce the double zigzag seam for knits:

1. Adjust the machine for a zigzag stitch of narrow width and short length.

2. With right sides together and raw edges aligned, zigzag the seam. Guide the fabric slightly to the left of the machine's stitching guide so that the left edge of the zigzag stitch falls at the ⅝" seam line.

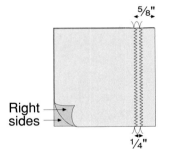

3. Add a second line of zigzag stitching approximately ¼" to the right of the first stitching. This second stitching holds the two seam edges together and prevents the edges from curling. Trim the seam allowance close to the second line of stitching.

Blindhem Seam

Here's a seam that is decorative as well as functional. Use a sewing machine blindhem stitch to scallop the seam edge. This stitch makes four straight stitches followed by one zigzag stitch.

To make the blindhem stitch:

1. Trim the seam allowance to ¼" prior to stitching the seam.

2. With right sides together and raw edges aligned, place the bulk of the fabric to the *right* of the presser foot. *This is contrary to the normal position for stitching, when the majority of the fabric is placed to the left of the presser foot.*

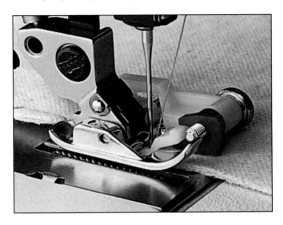

3. Adjust the machine for a blindhem stitch with a wide stitch width and a normal stitch length.

4. Stitch the seam. The straightstitch should fall along the ¼" seam line, while the zigzag stitch should fall off the fabric edge, drawing the fabric in and creating scallops.

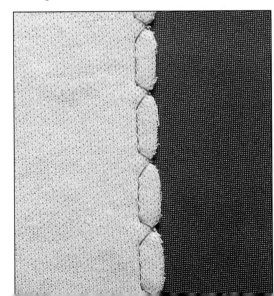

Serger Seams

Use your serger to help you stitch neat, durable lingerie seams. Depending on your lingerie project, select a 3-thread or a 3/4-thread overlock stitch.

The *3-thread overlock seam* is best for sheer knits and lightweight woven fabrics. Use only the *right* needle and a narrow stitch width.

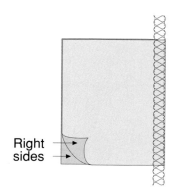

Right sides

The *3/4-thread overlock seam* is best for cotton knits and medium-weight woven fabrics. Use woolly nylon thread for a soft, comfortable seam, especially when you are working with knits.

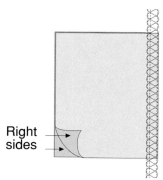

Right sides

Adding Lace

Lace is the focal point of many lingerie garments. Applying lace to a camisole like the one in the photograph below requires mitering the lace at both inward and outward corners. The fabric has been removed from behind the lace for additional detail and accent.

Here's how to work with these lace accents on both knit and woven fabrics.

Adding Edging Lace to Knit Fabrics

To add lace to a straight garment edge:

1. Place the lace, right side up, on the right side of the fabric, aligning the scalloped edge of the lace with the fabric's cut edge.

2. Temporarily "baste" the lace in place with sewing tape, liquid adhesive, or a fabric glue stick. These positioning aids allow the lace to remain perfectly straight as you stitch, preventing the dimples or drawn edges that sometimes result when pins are used.

3. Set your machine for a zigzag stitch of medium width and medium length. Stitch along the straight edge of the lace.

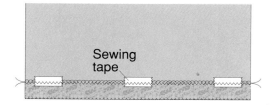

Sewing tape

4. Trim the fabric behind the lace using an appliqué scissors. Position the pelican-shaped blade under the fabric, beveling the scissors, and then trim.

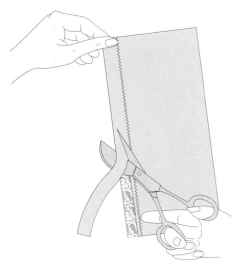

Adding Edging Lace to a Curved Edge

Applying edging lace to a curved edge can be a little tricky. Since the outer curve of the lace is slightly longer than the edge of the garment, the edge of the lace may buckle if sufficient length isn't allowed at the curve. Instead of pinning or gluing the lace to the fabric prior to stitching, "pin" it in place using your fingers. Use this technique to add lace to the outer edge of the Patternless Wrap Slip on page 80.

To apply edging lace to a curved edge:

1. Work with a small section (several inches long) at one time. Allow a small amount of slack in the lace. Position the lace close to the fabric edge and then use your fingers to hold the lace against the fabric several inches in front of the presser foot.

2. Stitch the area that you have "finger-pinned." Reposition your fingers and continue stitching, making sure to allow a slight bit of slack in the lace, until lace has been joined to the entire curved area. The extra lace will be eased to the fabric during stitching, and the lace will remain smooth and flat on the finished garment.

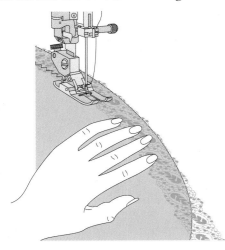

Adding Edging Lace to Woven Fabrics

Because woven lingerie fabrics are generally cut on the bias, it is easy to stretch or distort the edges of the garment during construction. Here is a hint to prevent this from happening.

1. Reposition the cut garment piece, right side up, on top of the pattern.

2. Pin or baste the lace to the fabric, using the paper pattern to ensure that the garment piece retains its original size and shape. Keep the garment positioned over the pattern until the lace is completely pinned or basted to the garment piece.

3. Adjust the machine for a zigzag stitch of narrow width and very short length, resembling a narrow satin stitch. Using this zigzag when stitching the lace to the fabric secures the edges of the fabric and prevents them from raveling.

4. Stitch the lace to the garment, following the same techniques used for adding lace to knit fabrics. Trim the excess fabric behind the lace.

Turning Corners with Mitered Lace Edging

Now that you know how to add lace to straight and curved edges, let's tackle those inward and outward corners often found on slips, gowns, and camisoles. Adding lace to these areas is easy if you have a little mitering know-how. Simply shape the lace to match the garment before stitching.

To miter outer corners:

1. On the right side of the garment piece, place the lace, right side up, along the edge of the fabric, with one scalloped edge even with the edge of the fabric. Stop at the outer corner. Pin or tape the lace in place. Place a pin through the lace at the outer corner.

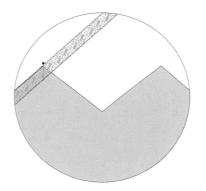

2. Fold the lace back on itself and reposition the lace so that the scalloped edge aligns with the next fabric edge, mitering the corner.

Pin or tape the lace in place, following the curve of the garment.

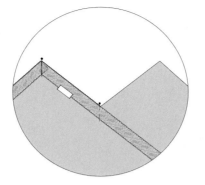

3. Following Steps 3 and 4 on page 69, stitch the lace to the edges of the garment.

Following Steps 3 and 4 on page 69

> ### Note from Nancy
> Remember, when you are working with woven fabrics, place the garment piece on the paper pattern after the lace has been pinned or taped to be sure that the edges have not been stretched out of shape.

To miter inner corners:

1. Fold the lace in half, with right sides together and the scalloped edge at the top, matching and stacking the motifs of the lace.

2. At the fold, pin through both lace layers at a 45° angle.

3. Unfold the mitered lace corner and align the lace with the next edge of the garment. The upper edge of the pinned corner should be exactly at the center point of the garment corner.

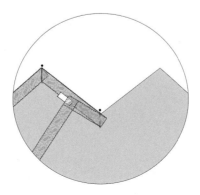

4. If necessary, adjust the pin so that the lace fits the contour of the garment. Pin or tape the lace to the garment.

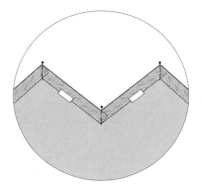

5. Following Steps 3 and 4 of "Adding Edging Lace to Knit Fabrics" on page 68, stitch the lace to the edge of the garment.

6. From the right side of the garment, topstitch through the center of each miter. Trim excess lace from the wrong side.

Following Steps 3 and 4 of "Adding Edging Lace to Knit Fabrics" on page 68

Hemming the Garment with Insertion Lace

Here's a lace application that hems the garment and adds a touch of elegance in one easy sewing step.

1. Press the hem to the wrong side of the garment. If necessary, use pins, tape, or liquid adhesive to hold the hem in place.

2. On the right side of the garment, use pins, tape, or fabric glue to baste the lace in place, centering the lace along the hemline.

3. Zigzag along both sides of the lace.

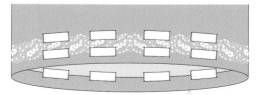

4. Working from the wrong side of the garment, trim the excess fabric behind the lace.

Applying Elastic

My basic philosophy in stitching elastic to lingerie is "less is best." Too many stitches can cut the elastic yarns and cause the elastic to lose its stretch, so the fewer the stitches used in applying the elastic, the longer the elastic will last—plus it saves time!

What type of elastic should you use? Apply traditional lingerie elastic at the waistline and leg openings of panties and other lingerie garments or use stretch lace for an elastic finish that is both functional and decorative.

Applying Traditional Lingerie Elastic

For a traditional edge finish, use picot-edged lingerie elastic at the waistline and the leg openings of panties and other lingerie garments. This elastic comes in various colors to match the lingerie fabric and is available in widths of ¼" and ½".

The seam where the cut ends of the elastic are joined is sometimes less attractive than the remainder of the garment. Take a look at expensive ready-to-wear lingerie and you'll find that the seam is often covered with a bit of ribbon that conceals the joining, plus adds an attractive touch. Here's how to duplicate that look on your next lingerie project.

To conceal the seam with ribbon:

1. Stitch or serge the side seams of the garment to which the elastic will be attached.

2. Cut the elastic 2" shorter than the wearer's waist or leg measurement.

3. To join the ends of the elastic:
- Cut a 2" length of ½"-wide ribbon in a color that coordinates with the garment.
- Butt the ends of the elastic together and center them over the ribbon, approximately ¼" from one end of the ribbon, leaving a portion of the ribbon extending below the elastic. (The excess ribbon will be trimmed after the elastic is joined to the garment.)
- Zigzag the ends of the elastic securely to the ribbon.

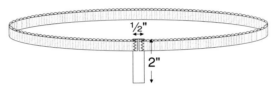

- Wrap the ribbon up and around the elastic, concealing the stitching.

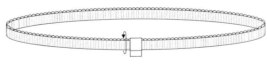

4. To apply the elastic to the garment:
- Quarter-mark both the elastic and the garment opening.
- With the *wrong* side of the elastic facing the *right* side of the garment, match the quarter marks. Pin the elastic to the garment, placing the picot edge of the elastic even with the cut edge of the fabric.
- Stitch the elastic to the garment with a narrow zigzag stitch or multi-zigzag stitch, stretching the elastic to fit.
- Trim the excess fabric behind the elastic. Trim the excess ribbon extending below the lower edge of the elastic.

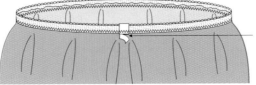

Trim excess ribbon.

Applying Stretch Lace

Stretch lace, available in widths of ⅜" and ¾", is perfect for panty waistline and leg openings. In addition, this very feminine elastic is also available in wider widths, from 2" to 4". Use the wider lace to provide greater comfort at the waistlines of panties and slips.

To apply stretch lace:

1. Cut the stretch lace according to the guidelines given with your pattern. Or cut the lace 2" shorter than the measurement of the waistline or leg.

2. Set your machine for a zigzag stitch of medium width and length. With *wrong* sides together and raw edges even, zigzag the ends of the elastic together.

3. Finger-press the seam to one side. For reinforcement, topstitch the pressed seam using a wide zigzag stitch.

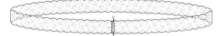

4. Apply the stretch lace to the garment.
• Quarter-mark both the elastic and the garment opening.
• With the *wrong* side of the lace facing the *right* side of the garment, align the quarter marks.

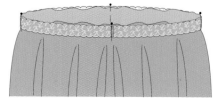

Note from Nancy
Most lingerie patterns include only a ¼" seam allowance. If the pattern calls for a narrow elastic and you're using a 2"-wide stretch lace, align the scalloped edge of the stretch lace with the cut edge of the fabric. When the lower edge of the lace is stitched to the garment and the excess fabric is trimmed, the garment will have proportions comparable to that of the original pattern, regardless of the width of the elastic you use.

• Set your machine for a zigzag stitch. For knit fabrics, use a stitch of medium width and length; for woven fabrics, use a stitch of narrow width and short length. Zigzag along the lower edge of the stretch lace, stretching the elastic to meet the fabric.

5. Trim the excess fabric behind the lace.

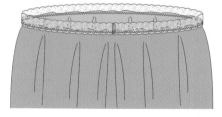

Applying Clear Elastic

To apply clear elastic:

1. Cut the ½"-wide clear elastic 2" longer than the pattern indicates. (The extra 2" provides a 1" tail at each end to grasp and stretch the elastic as you stitch it to the fabric.)

2. With a ballpoint pen, mark 1" from each cut end of the elastic. Between the two end marks, divide the elastic into quarters and mark each quarter point with the ball-point pen. (Normally, ballpoint ink isn't recommended for marking sewing projects. But in the case of clear elastic, ballpoint ink is the only mark that will show.)

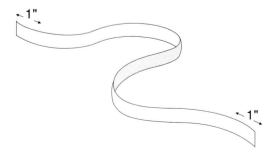

3. Using pins, quarter-mark the fabric.

4. With the elastic facing the *wrong* side of the fabric and long edges aligned, pin the elastic and garment together, matching quarter marks. Leave the 1" tails of elastic extending at each end.

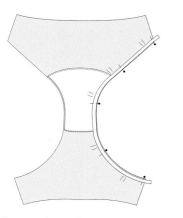

5. Set the machine for a wide zigzag stitch of medium length.

6. Zigzag the elastic along the inner edge, stretching the elastic to fit the fabric. (Minimal stretching is all that's normally required since the garment is usually only slightly larger than the elastic.) Stitching along the inner edge makes it easier to turn and encase the elastic.

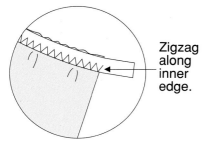

Zigzag along inner edge.

7. Stitch the side seams of the garment.

8. Encase the elastic by folding the elastic and fabric to the wrong side of the garment.

9. From the right side of the fabric, straightstitch or zigzag ¼" from the folded edge through all the layers.

Note from Nancy
Instead of straightstitching or zigzagging this final row of stitching, try using a straightstitch with a double needle. The two rows of topstitching remain an equal distance apart on the right side, and the bobbin thread builds in stretch as it zigzags between the two top threads. It's a great alternative stitch for activewear.

Adding the Finishing Touches

Straps

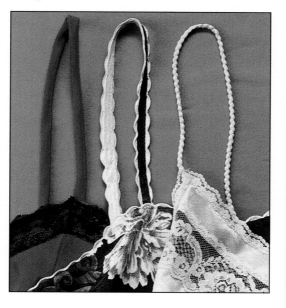

Here are several ideas for adding a one-of-a-kind look to your garments with straps you can custom-make in mere minutes. Choose from a simple stretch strap, a turned bias strap, or a delicate picot-edged strap. They're easy!

Stretch Straps

A crosswise strip of tricot and a single line of machine stitching are all you need to make this simple, attractive lingerie strap.

1. Cut two crosswise tricot strips, 1" to 1½" wide. Cut the strips slightly longer than needed for the completed straps. The strips will be stretched as they are sewn, and the added length allows room for grasping and pulling the fabric.

2. Set your sewing machine for a zigzag stitch of wide width and medium length. Pull one tricot strip taut. The edges will curl toward the center.

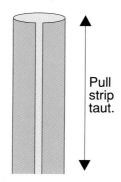

Pull strip taut.

3. Stitch over the curled fabric. The zigzag stitches will "couch" the fabric, stitching on each side of the fabric rather than through it. In one step, the edges of the strap are clean-finished and stretch is built into the strap. Repeat to finish both tricot strips.

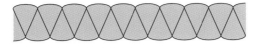

Quick-Turn Straps

Special turning tools make this strap a snap! Both the Narrow Loop Turner and the Fasturn help you turn tubes right side out in one simple motion.

To make the straps:

1. For each strap, cut a strip of fabric 1½" wide and slightly longer than the desired length. (With knit fabrics, cut the strip on the lengthwise grain. With woven fabrics, cut the strip on the bias.) This size strip will make a finished ⅜"-wide strap.

2. With right sides together and long edges aligned, fold the strip in half and straightstitch down the center of the strip. Center the presser foot on the fabric so that an equal amount of fabric extends on either side of the needle.

3. To turn the strap, insert a Narrow Loop Turner inside the stitched strap. Catch the fabric at the end of the strap by pushing the latch hook through the fabric. Pull the turner back through the strap.

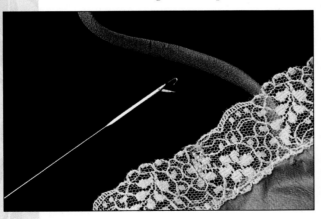

or

Thread the stitched strap onto a ⅛" or ³⁄₁₆" Fasturn cylinder. Wrap and fold the fabric end tightly over the end of the cylinder. Insert the pigtail hook end of the Fasturn through the cylinder; twist the end to the right to catch the fabric. Gently pull the hook back through the cylinder to turn the tube. Release the hook by twisting it to the left.

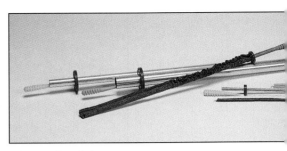

Picot-edged Accents

This robe and gown feature simple yet elegant picot-edged accents on the straps, facing, and front band. This embellishment, ideal for woven fabrics, is easily made with the blindhem stitch on your sewing machine.

Making Picot-edged Straps

1. Make a quick-turn strap.

2. Press the turned strap so that the seam is centered.

3. On the right side of the pressed strap, center a ¼"-wide satin ribbon of contrasting color.

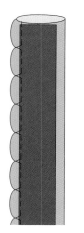

4. Adjust the machine for a blindhem stitch of medium to wide width and medium length. (Specific settings for the stitch width and length may vary, depending on the desired look. Experiment on a scrap before stitching the straps for the garment.)

5. Turn the balance wheel by hand until the needle "zigs" to the left. Position the pressed strap under the presser foot to the right of the needle. Stitch along the left edge of the strap. The straightstitching should secure the edge of the ribbon, while the "zig" should go off the folded edge. This draws in the edge at each "zig," creating a picot.

6. Repeat the process on the remaining side of the strap, aligning the "zigs" so that they are directly opposite those on the first side of the strap. Repeat to complete second strap.

Adding Picot-edged Trim

Picot-edged trim can be added to a front band or facing with a minimum of effort.

1. Cut several 1¾"-wide *bias* fabric strips (depending upon the length desired for the picot-edged trim). With right sides together and raw edges aligned, join the short edges of the bias strips. Press the seams open.

2. Adjust your sewing machine for a blindhem stitch of medium width.

3. With *wrong* sides together and long edges aligned, place the strip under the presser foot with the folded edge at the *left*. Stitch ¼" from the fold, allowing the "zig" to stitch off the folded edge.

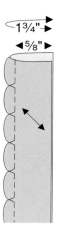

4. Prepare the facing band or the facing according to the instructions on the pattern guide sheet.

Timesaving Notions
When you're working with slippery silk-like fabrics, the seam allowance sometimes refuses to stay pressed under. Use a fabric glue stick to temporarily baste the seam allowance in place before you stitch. The glue washes out completely and is nontoxic and odorless.

Timesaving Notions
Wonder Thread is an ideal way to join the picot-edged trim to the garment with invisible stitching. This new thread is thinner than regular nylon monofilament thread and works well on delicate lingerie fabrics.

5. Pin or glue-baste the picot-edged trim to the right side of the *front band,* aligning raw edges. With right sides together and raw edges aligned, pin the front band to the garment. (The picot-edged trim will be sandwiched between the two fabric pieces.) Stitch, using a ⅝" seam allowance.

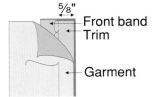

Or, if you are using a *facing,* pin or glue-baste the picot-edged trim to the right side of the facing. With right sides together, pin the facing to the garment. Stitch, using a ⅝" seam allowance.

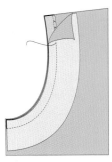

6. Trim the excess fabric from the seam. Finish the raw edges of the seam by serging or zigzagging the edges together.

Shadow Appliqué Techniques

Shadow appliqués make lovely accents on lingerie. To create the see-through effect of the shadow appliqué, use this simple stitching and trimming approach.

1. Choose a sheer fabric such as bridal illusion, organdy, or sheer tricot for the upper fabric. For the shadow fabric, choose a solid-colored fabric a bit brighter than you want the final appliqué to appear. The upper layer of sheer fabric will tone down the color.

2. Using a marking pen, trace the appliqué design onto the sheer fabric.

3. To stitch the shadow appliqué:

• Place small sections of the shadow appliqué fabric under the areas that will have the shadow effect; pin in place. Back with Wash-Away stabilizer.

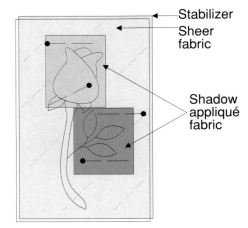

• To attach the shadow fabric, straight-stitch around the design, using a short stitch length (20 stitches per inch).

• Working from the back of the design, trim the excess shadow fabric and stabilizer outside the stitching. To cut very close to the stitching line, use an appliqué scissors or bevel the blades of a standard scissors.

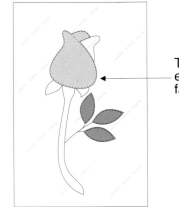

4. To attach the shadow appliqué to the right side of the garment:

• Create a fabric "sandwich" by placing the shadow appliqué design on the right side of the garment and then backing the garment fabric with another layer of water-soluble stabilizer. Pin around the entire design.

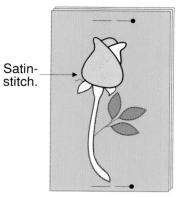

Satin-stitch.

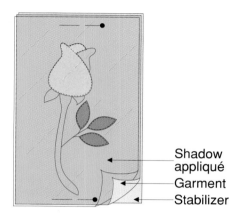

Shadow appliqué
Garment
Stabilizer

• Straightstitch around the outer edges of the design where the garment fabric will be cut away.

• Working from the wrong side of the garment, use an appliqué scissors to trim the excess garment fabric from the area covered by the sheer shadow appliqué. Be careful not to clip into the overlay fabric.

• On the right side of the garment, trim the sheer fabric outside the appliqué, being careful not to clip any threads.

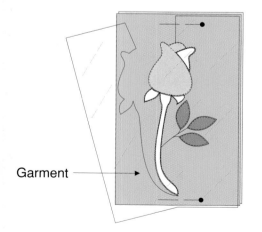

Garment

• Position another layer of water-soluble stabilizer behind the appliqué.

• Satin-stitch around the entire appliqué. The more detailed the appliqué, the narrower the width of the satin stitching should be.

"Antique" Lace

Add a nostalgic touch to your next lingerie project by embellishing lace. Use your sewing machine and free-motion embroidery techniques to enhance white or ecru lace with several shades of thread.

1. Pin or glue lace to a large sheet of water-soluble stabilizer. (Generally, the lace pieces to be embroidered are not large enough to fill the area of an embroidery hoop, and the stabilizer provides a large surface for the hoop to grasp.)

Note from Nancy
Rather than pinning the lace to the Wash-Away, try temporarily basting it in position with Insta-Pin or a fabric glue stick. After you've added the embroidery, dip the lace in water to dissolve the stabilizer and adhesive.

2. Adjust the sewing machine for free-motion embroidery.

- Set the machine for a straight stitch.
- Lower the feed dogs and remove the presser foot.
- Use cotton or rayon embroidery thread in a coordinating or contrasting color in the needle and in the bobbin.

3. Place the stabilizer-backed lace securely in a wooden embroidery hoop. With the fabric flat against the bed of the machine, place the hoop under the presser foot bar.

4. Hold the top thread with your left hand. Take one stitch, turning the balance wheel by hand to bring up the bobbin thread. Pull the thread to the top side and toward the back of the presser foot.

5. Lower the presser bar. *This is extremely important!* If you do not lower the presser bar, the upper thread will be under no tension, and the threads will knot and jam on the underside of the fabric instead of making smooth stitches. When you're stitching without a presser foot, it's difficult to tell if the bar has been lowered. Check to be sure!

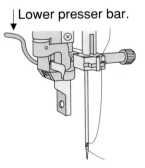

Lower presser bar.

6. Holding both threads firmly, stitch in place several times to secure the threads. If possible, stop with the machine needle in the down position. Clip the excess thread tails.

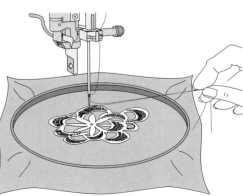

7. Embroider the open areas of the lace with a straightstitch.

- Imagining the embroidery hoop as the face of a clock, position your hands at two o'clock and ten o'clock. Stitch, moving the hoop to follow the shape of the lace. Move the hoop from side to side and forward and backward, but do not turn it like a steering wheel. You must keep the twelve o'clock position at the top of the hoop at all times.

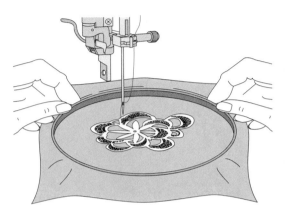

- Move the hoop slowly, but stitch at a fairly fast speed.
- Try using several shades of the same color thread to add dimension and a shadowing effect. Begin with the darkest color and then move to lighter ones.

8. Remove the stabilizer-backed lace from the hoop. Dip the lace in water to dissolve the stabilizer and adhesive. Let the lace dry.

9. Attach the lace to the lingerie.

Creating Your Own Lingerie

Now it's time to put these techniques to use. Choose from six simple lingerie projects—they're luxurious!

Panties

Making a pair of panties requires only a small amount of fabric, a minimal amount of sewing time, and a little sewing savvy. Follow these easy directions to quickly sew or serge a pair of panties.

Panties with Lined Crotch

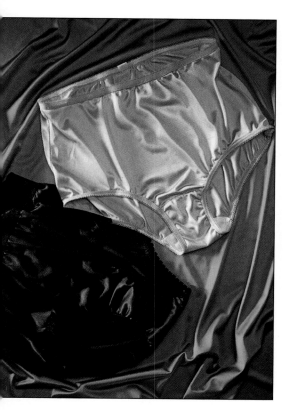

A panty pattern usually includes a front piece, a back piece, and two crotch pieces. Cut one crotch piece of fashion fabric and one of 100% cotton interlock or jersey knit for wearing comfort.

To make the panties:

1. Place the two crotch pieces with right sides together. Sandwich the front of the panty between the two crotch pieces, with the right side of the panty front next to the right side of the fashion fabric crotch piece.

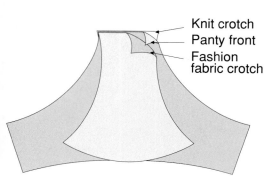

Knit crotch
Panty front
Fashion fabric crotch

2. Serge or sew a ¼" seam.

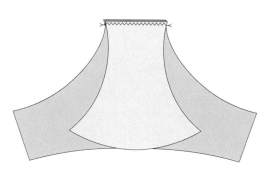

3. To join the panty back to the crotch pieces:

• With the right side of the panty back facing the right side of the outer (fashion fabric) crotch piece, pin the pieces together.

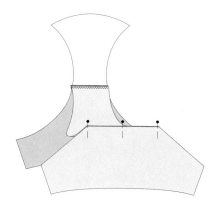

• Align the panties with right sides together, matching the crotch seam lines and folding the outer (fashion fabric) crotch piece between the front and back. Wrap the crotch lining completely around

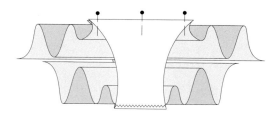

the panties. With the right side of the crotch lining facing the wrong side of the panty back, pin the seam, placing the heads of the pins toward the cut edges to make it easy to remove them during stitching.

• Stitch through all the layers, completely enclosing all the raw edges.

• Turn the panties right side out. Stitch the side seams.

4. Apply elastic to the leg openings and waistline of the panties.

One-piece Panties

Now that you know how to stitch the crotch on a traditional pair of panties, try another alternative. Instead of using the pattern as it comes in the envelope, convert the pattern to one piece for a smoother fit and streamlined sewing. Converting the pattern is easy, since all three pattern pieces have similar grain lines. The only disadvantage is that the panties take slightly more fabric.

The basic change for this technique must be made before the garment is cut out. Here's how to adapt your pattern.

1. Cut out the pattern pieces for the panty front, back, and crotch. Align the stitching line for the crotch pattern with the stitching lines for the panty front and back. (You will probably notice that at the sides of the crotch seam, the seam is slightly greater than ¼". Don't worry! The pattern includes sufficient fullness at the leg opening to provide for this slight overlap.) Cut out the entire pattern as one piece.

2. Using the one-piece pattern, cut the panty from the fashion fabric.

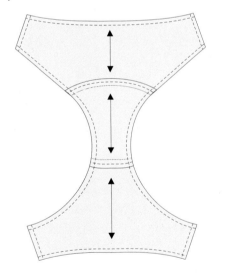

3. Using the original crotch pattern, cut a separate crotch piece from 100% cotton jersey knit. Straighten the front and the back seam allowances slightly to correspond to that of the new one-piece pattern.

4. At the front and back edges of the cotton knit crotch piece, press or finger-press ¼" seam allowances to the wrong side.

5. Position the cotton knit crotch lining on the wrong side of the panty. Zigzag or straightstitch the edges in place. Stitch the side seams.

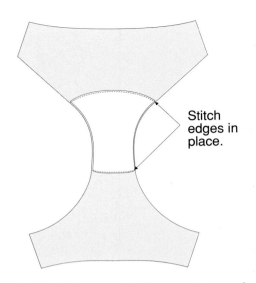

Stitch edges in place.

6. Apply elastic to the leg openings and waistline of the panty.

Patternless Wrap Slip

Here's another design idea—a patternless wrap slip with no side seams. Wear it underneath garments with a slit at the hemline and you'll never see a slip peeking through.

The slip can be made of either woven or knit fabric. Start with a rectangle of fabric, follow these easy directions to curve the lower edge, finish its outer edges with lace, and complete its waistline with elastic.

1. Choose your fabrics and supplies:
  • *¾ yard of lingerie fabric*, either knit

or woven. The finished slip will be 27" long. For a longer or shorter slip, adjust the amount of fabric. If your hip measurement is more than 40" and the fabric is 45" wide, purchase 1½ yards of fabric.

• *Lingerie elastic or stretch lace*: a length 2" shorter than your waistline measurement.

• *2½ to 3½ yards of ½"-wide edging lace*, depending on the size of the slip.

2. Cut a rectangle 27" long by the width of your hipline measurement plus 6". For example, if your hipline measures 38", the rectangle would measure 27" x 44" (38"+6").

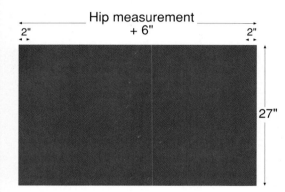

Hip measurement + 6"

2"   2"

27"

3. At the top of the rectangle, place a mark or a short nip 2" from each end. These nips provide matching points for the wrap overlap.

4. To form a curve at the lower edges of the rectangle:

• Measure up 10" from one bottom corner; mark.

• From the same corner, measure 3" at a 45° angle; mark.

• Measure 7" from the same corner along the bottom; mark.

• Connect the three points, forming a gentle curve. Fold the fabric rectangle in half crosswise, aligning the short edges. Following the curved line, cut through both layers of fabric.

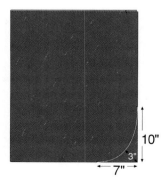

10"

3"

7"

5. Using a narrow zigzag stitch, attach the lace along the side and hem edges. "Finger-pin" to position the lace, following the techniques on page 69.

6. Matching the nips or markings along the upper edge, overlap the ends of the waistline. (The total overlap will be 4".) Pin the overlap in place and machine-baste. If you are using a woven fabric, serge or zigzag the raw edges of the waistline to prevent raveling.

Overlap.

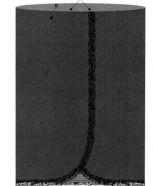

7. Apply the waistline elastic, following the techniques on page 71.

Stretch Lace Waistline Insert

One of the most intriguing parts of sewing is making design changes to create garments that reflect your personal touch. The pattern for this nightgown is altered to include a 4" stretch lace insert, making the gown fitted at the waistline.

The gown is soft and luxurious-looking, and the stretch lace makes the gown so comfortable to wear. A similar elastic insert could be added at the waistline of a slip or camisole.

1. To modify the pattern, locate the waistline on the bodice pattern piece. Measure and add half the width of the lace below the waistline. On the skirt pattern piece, add half the width of the lace above the waistline. (The ⅝" seam allowance is eliminated on both the skirt and bodice.)

> ### Note from Nancy
> *If the waistline isn't marked on the pattern, hold the pattern up to your body and mark the position of your waist. Then draw a line at right angles to the straight of grain 2" below the waistline. This added 2" allows room for movement.*

2. Use the modified pattern pieces to cut the garment.

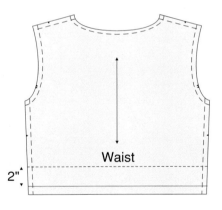

3. Cut a length of 2"- to 4"-wide stretch lace that measures approximately 2" smaller than your waistline measurement. Check the length before you cut by placing the elastic around your waist to make sure it is comfortable.

> ### Note from Nancy
> *Make sure the stretch lace fits over your head and shoulders so that you can get in and out of the garment. Before cutting, pin it together and try to slip it over your head and shoulders. When you're sure it's the correct size, cut the lace.*

4. On both the bodice and skirt sections, serge or stitch all except one of the garment's side seams.

5. Check to see whether the lace will stretch enough to meet the fabric. If not, gather the bodice edge before joining the lace to the bodice.

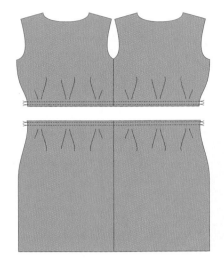

6. Apply the stretch lace to the garment's bodice section.

- Quarter-mark both the elastic and the bodice. With the *wrong* side of the lace next to the *right* side of the bodice, match the quarter marks. Place the lower edge of the lace *even* with the cut edge of the bodice. (This assures that the finished garment will retain its original length.) Pin at the quarter marks.

- With right sides together, align the upper edge of the lace with the lower cut edge of the bodice.

- Pull the gathering threads so that the bodice meets the stretched lace.

• Zigzag along the upper edge of the stretch lace, stretching the elastic to meet the fabric. With *knit fabrics,* use a medium zigzag stitch. With *woven fabrics,* use a narrow zigzag stitch.

• Trim excess fabric behind the lace.

7. Repeat Step 6 to join the stretch lace to the garment's skirt section.

8. Stitch the remaining side seam and complete the gown, following the pattern instructions.

Activewear Elastic Applications

This sport bra and brief set were made quickly and easily, with only a few seams and using easy elastic applications.

1. Choose your fabric and elastics:

• Select a cotton/lycra stretch jersey with at least 75% stretch. If desired, you may line the fabric with a swimwear lining of comparable stretch.

• Look for sheer elastic, a soft and supple 1½"-wide elastic made of nylon-covered spandex threads, to apply at the waistline of the brief and the lower edge of the sport bra.

• Use clear elastic around the neckline, armholes, and leg openings.

2. Referring to the panty techniques on page 79, join the crotch seams of the brief. Stitch the shoulder seams of the sport bra. DO NOT join the side seams at this time.

3. Apply the clear elastic to the leg openings and armholes.

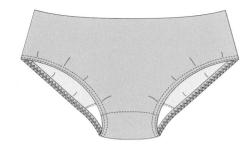

4. At the waist edges of the bra and brief, apply the sheer elastic, using the techniques described for stretch lace on page 72.

Lace Laundry Bag

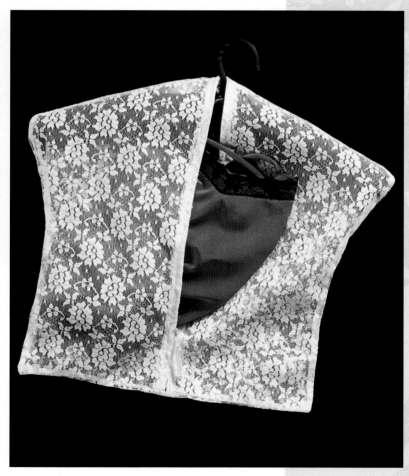

A lacy laundry bag is a tasteful way to store all those luxurious lingerie garments while they're waiting to be laundered. Choose a polyester or nylon allover lace fabric to create the bag—a great gift for a birthday, a shower, Mother's Day, or any other special occasion.

Timesaving Notions
I prefer to use basting tape instead of pins when applying a zipper. Place the tape, which has a temporary adhesive on both sides, within one of the seam allowances. Peel off the protective paper covering. Align the right side of the zipper tape with the folded center edge and finger-press the zipper to the basting tape. This will prevent the zipper from shifting while it is being stitched.

1. Make the pattern for the back of the laundry bag by tracing around the outer edges of a hanger. Extend the pattern to the desired finished length of the laundry bag; add ¼" to ½" seam allowances all around the pattern.

2. Prepare a pattern for the front of the laundry bag to allow for a zipper opening by folding the pattern for the back in half lengthwise. Trace, adding a ⅝" seam allowance at the center front for the zipper.

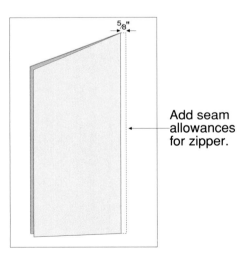

Add seam allowances for zipper.

3. From a single layer of the lace yardage, cut the bag back. Fold the remaining lace in half and cut two pieces for the bag front.

4. To apply the zipper to the center front opening:

• Press under the seam allowances on the center front edges. Align the right side of the zipper to the folded seam allowance and position the zipper teeth next to the pressed-under edge.

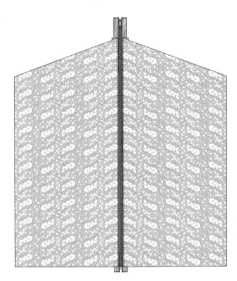

• Use a zipper foot to topstitch the zipper in place.

> ***Note from Nancy***
> *I always use a zipper slightly longer than the opening to which it will be applied, extending the extra length at the top of the opening. Then I don't have to worry about stitching around the zipper tab or the grommet at the top of the zipper. After the zipper is inserted, pull the zipper tab down into the zipper opening. Stitch the seams and then trim the excess length.*

5. With right sides together and raw edges aligned, place the front and back pieces together. To stabilize the top seams, pin a matching piece of ribbon or bias fabric along the seam line.

6. Beginning at the zipper opening, serge or stitch the ribbon and the seams together across the top. Continue stitching along the side seams and across the lower edge. Stitch the remaining top seam, leaving an opening at the zipper for inserting the hanger.

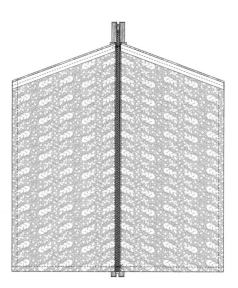

7. Trim the excess zipper length. Turn the laundry bag right side out; insert the hanger. Remove the hanger during laundering.

Note from Nancy

Ordinarily we sort laundry by color, keeping light fabrics separate from dark ones. When you launder lingerie, go one step further. Some of your lingerie may be made from synthetic fibers and other pieces from natural fibers. Even though they're the same color, they should NOT be washed together. Synthetics, especially nylon, attract dirt from natural fibers. If the two are washed together, the synthetic fabrics will acquire a dingy or yellow cast. So wash garments of natural fibers in one load and garments of synthetic fibers in another.

Speed Tailoring

Believe it or not, it's easy to make a tailored jacket in a weekend with the speed tailoring techniques outlined in this chapter. By replacing traditional hand-worked shaping with fusible interfacings, you can achieve professional results in a fraction of the sewing time. You'll love the ease of sewing and the professional look and fit of your speed-tailored jacket.

Tailoring with Fusible Interfacings

The key to speed tailoring is choosing the correct weights of fusible interfacings. You need two weights of interfacing when sewing a lined jacket: one for shaping the body of the jacket and a second for crisper shaping of the lapel.

Choosing the Correct Fusibles

Interfacing for the Jacket Body

For allover interfacing, choose a soft, drapable fusible that will add support, shape, and stability without adding stiffness. The average jacket will require 1½ yards of the body interfacing.

Interfacing for the Lapels

The interfacing used on the lapels must have greater weight than the allover interfacing and have both crosswise stretch and lengthwise stability.

Timesaving Notions
For allover interfacing, I use Pellon Sof-Shape, a versatile bias interfacing perfect for linen, wool, gabardine, corduroy, and even cotton velvet. Other fusible interfacings suitable for this purpose include Armo Fusi-Form Lightweight, Suit-Maker, and Shape-Up Lightweight.

Using such an interfacing eliminates the tedious padstitching done by hand that was once common to tailoring. You'll be using only a small amount (½ yard or less) of this crisper interfacing.

> ***Note from Nancy***
> *My favorite crisp interfacing is Pellon Pel-Aire, the fusible used for lapel shaping by manufacturers of ready-to-wear garments. Pel-Aire has the two key characteristics needed for lapel interfacing: crosswise stretch and lengthwise stability. Similar products are Armo Fusi-Form Suitweight, Armo Form-Flex Nonwoven, and Shape-Up Suitweight.*

Making a Fusible Interfacing Test Swatch

Before cutting out and fusing your interfacing, make a test swatch to determine the fusing time needed and whether the interfacing is suitable for your fabric. This is especially important if you're using a new interfacing or fabric, or are combining an interfacing and fabric for the first time.

To make a test swatch:

1. Cut a 4" square of both the fusible interfacing and the fabric.

2. Place the wrong side of the fabric next to the resin-treated side of the interfacing.

3. Place another small square of fabric at one corner, between the fashion fabric and interfacing.

• Position the test swatch on the ironing board with the nonresin side up.

• Fuse the interfacing for 10 to 15 seconds, using a steam iron at wool setting.

4. Let the test swatch cool; then test for proper fusing by pulling on a corner. If you can easily separate the interfacing from the fabric, increase the fusing time, pressure, and temperature.

5. Check the appearance of both the right and wrong sides of the interfaced test square. If the interfacing shows as a ridge on the right side of the fabric, or if the interfaced fabric feels uncomfortably stiff, choose a lighter weight interfacing and test again.

Making Pattern Pieces for Interfacing

When you are making tailored garments, every pattern piece cut from the outer fabric is shaped and stabilized with fusible interfacing. Some areas of the jacket are fully interfaced, some are partially interfaced, and some are stabilized with two layers of fusible interfacing.

Full Interfacing

In ready-to-wear jackets, fusible interfacing is used to shape the entire section of these pieces:

Jacket front   Upper collar
Side front   Under collar
Front facing   Pocket flaps
Back facing

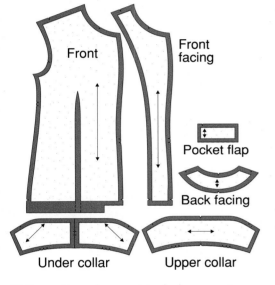

Front

Front facing

Pocket flap

Back facing

Under collar   Upper collar

If the pattern does not include separate pattern pieces for interfacing, make your own, following these guidelines.

1. Duplicate the pattern pieces.

• Work on a surface padded with a tablecloth or a length of fabric.

• Place a length of waxed paper over the standard pattern piece.

• Set the sliding guide of a 6" seam gauge at ½". The original seam and hem allowances are ⅝" deep, so removing ½" will leave ⅛" of interfacing outside the seam line.

• Guide the outside corner of the seam gauge along the cutting line of the pattern. The outside corner and the sliding guide on the gauge will scratch the wax from the paper, leaving two marks: the original cutting line and the interfacing cutting line.

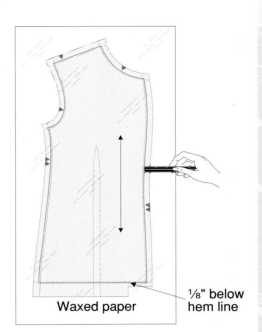

Waxed paper

⅛" below hem line

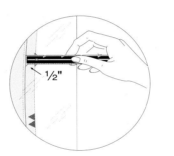

½"

2. Transfer the grain line from the pattern to the waxed paper interfacing pattern.

3. Cut out the interfacing, using the inner (½") line on the waxed paper pattern as the cutting line. Trim the interfacing from the dart areas.

Partial Interfacing

Upper Back

In the *upper back* of the jacket, only a partial interfacing is needed to support the shoulder area.

To make the interfacing pattern for the partially fused section of the jacket back:

1. Place the waxed paper over the jacket back pattern.

2. Begin approximately 2" below the underarm seam and trace a line that curves upward to a point on the center back seam line approximately 6" to 8" below the seam line at the neck.

3. Use the 6" seam gauge and guide the outside corner of the gauge along the cutting lines of the neck, shoulder, armhole, center back, and underarm.

Timesaving Notions
Cover the ironing board with an Appliqué Pressing Sheet before positioning the swatch. The nonstick surface protects the ironing board cover from the fusible web. (If by chance part of the web is fused to the pressing sheet, it will peel right off.)

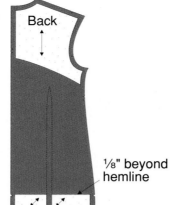

Back

⅛" beyond hemline

> ### Note from Nancy
> *If the outer fabric is lightweight, the fusible interfacing could leave a ridge on the right side of the fabric where the interfacing stops. If this happens, use a sew-in interfacing for the back interfacing ONLY. Machine-baste the interfacing to the jacket back at the shoulder and side seam lines.*

Hemlines

On the hemlines of the jacket's front, sides, and facings, the interfacing extends ⅛" into the hem allowance, giving a rounded edge and a tailored look to the hem. On the back hemline, sleeve hemlines, and sleeve vents, use the allover (lighter weight) interfacing for a similar tailored hemline.

To interface the hemlines and sleeve vents:

1. For the hemlines, cut several bias strips of interfacing the width of the hem plus ⅛". For the sleeve vents, cut the strips the width of the vent plus ⅛".

2. With the resin side of the interfacing against the wrong side of the garment piece, place the bias strips along the edges of the hem and vent allowances. Begin and end the placement ½" from the cut edges of the seams to minimize bulk.

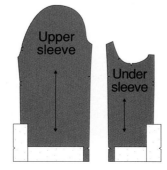

Upper sleeve

Under sleeve

Double Interfacing

In the roll line of the jacket's lapel and in the under collar, a second layer of interfacing is necessary to provide the shaping and stability without padstitching by hand. This is where I use the crisper interfacing.

Lapel Double Interfacing

For the second layer in the lapel area, make a second interfacing pattern piece from the jacket front pattern.

1. Place the waxed paper ⅛" inside the roll line—the diagonal line drawn on the jacket front that starts at the top button and extends into the under collar. (Usually this line is marked on the jacket front, although the roll-line position may change if the pattern is altered.)

> ### Note from Nancy
> *The second layer of interfacing is purposely placed ⅛" away from the roll line so that the garment will easily roll on the desired line.*

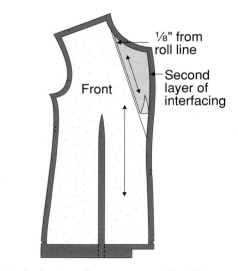

⅛" from roll line

Second layer of interfacing

Front

2. Mark the interfacing cutting line ⅛" into the seam allowance at the neck and outer edge of the lapel. Mark the interfacing grain line parallel to the jacket grain line.

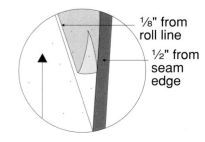

⅛" from roll line

½" from seam edge

(The second layer of interfacing will be cut with the straight of grain to provide maximum stability along the roll line.)

Under Collar Double Interfacing

The roll line continues from the neckline of the jacket into the under collar, requiring double interfacing on the under collar.

Cut *both* layers of interfacing from the crisp interfacing, since the under collar is crucial to the fit and shape of the jacket.

1. Following the guidelines listed under "Full Interfacing" on page 89, make an interfacing pattern from the original under collar pattern. Cut the first layer from the crisp interfacing.

2. Make a pattern for the second layer of interfacing.
  •Fold a piece of waxed paper in half.
  •Place the fold of the waxed paper at the pattern's center-back stitching line.
  •Draw the interfacing cutting line ⅛" from the roll line marked on the original pattern. Extend the interfacing ⅛" into the neckline seam allowance.

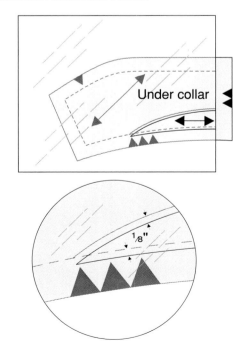

  •Mark the grain line *perpendicular* to the center back seam.

Note from Nancy
Usually the grain line of the interfacing follows the same grain line as the pattern. The second interfacing layers of the under collar and the lapel are the exceptions! The lengthwise grain has more stability and is positioned to give support to the under collar and the lapel.

3. Unfold the waxed paper. Cut one layer of interfacing from the complete interfacing pattern.

Successful Fusing

Full and Partial Interfacing Techniques

Although applying the interfacing takes a considerable block of time—approximately 30 minutes to fuse the interfacing to all the jacket pieces—it is one of the most important steps in contouring the jacket. Don't be in a hurry! For the best results, follow these simple guidelines.

1. With the fusible side of the interfacing against the wrong side of the fabric, steam-baste the interfacing to the fabric by touching the tip of your iron lightly at a few points around the seam edges. This prevents the interfacing from shifting as you fuse it.

2. Set your iron on steam at a wool setting. Cover the interfacing with a damp press cloth.

3. Fuse, pressing down firmly for a full 10 seconds. Fuse the interfacing, section by section, overlapping each section as you move to the next. *Do not slide the iron.*

4. Let the fabric cool.

Note from Nancy
Heat, time, and pressure are the key ingredients for success when fusing interfacing. Iron temperature and fusing time are easy to control, but proper pressure is a little more tricky to master. Try lowering the ironing board and leaning into the iron while fusing.

Double Interfacing Techniques

1. In the *lapel area*, fuse the second layer of interfacing to the lapel, following the fusing techniques previously described.

2. Fuse the interfacing to the *under collar.*
  •Fuse the first layer to the under collar, following the fusing techniques previously described.

• Stitch the center back seam. Press the seam flat and then press it open. Trim the seam allowance to ⅜".

• Fuse the second layer of interfacing to the *wrong* side of the under collar over the center back seam allowance.

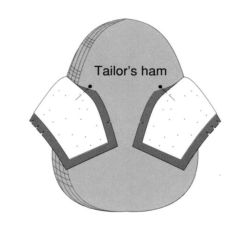

⅛" from roll line

3. After fusing the second layer of interfacing, shape the under collar.

• Create a permanent roll in the under collar by steaming it over a pressing ham. Roll the collar along the roll line and bend the collar to shape around the ham; pin in place.

Tailor's ham

• Steam (do not press) the collar.

• Let the collar cool and air dry before moving it. The roll line will be permanently shaped.

Construction of the Jacket Units

The fastest and most professional way to assemble a tailored jacket is to sew two separate units: an outer jacket unit and a lining unit, each with a front, back, sleeves, and collar. Following these step-by-step directions, it's easy to complete a jacket in a weekend or a few evening sewing sessions.

Outer jacket unit

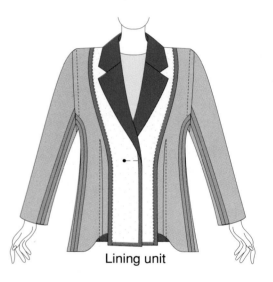

Lining unit

Assembling the Outer Jacket

If your sewing time is limited, take a few seconds to divide your project into work units. Below are possible project segments for the outer jacket unit.

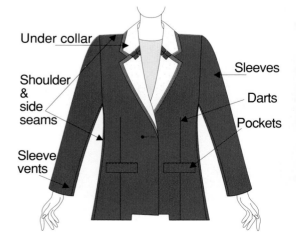

Under collar

Shoulder & side seams

Sleeve vents

Sleeves

Darts

Pockets

Darts

To construct the darts:

1. Sew the darts in the jacket front.

2. Using a tailor's ham to shape the curves, press the darts toward the center front.

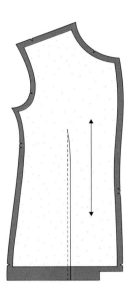

3. Stitch the front and side jacket pieces together. Press the seams flat and then press them open.

Patch Pockets

The secret to success in making patch pockets with beautiful corners is transparent tape—the same easy-to-remove tape you have tucked in your kitchen drawer. The tape serves a double purpose: it holds the fabric edges together as you sew, and it acts as a great stitching guide.

1. Miter the lower pocket corners.

•Along each side and the lower edge, mark a point 1¼" (twice the ⅝" seam width) from the corner.

•On the wrong side of the fabric, place transparent tape between the two marks, extending the tape ends as shown.

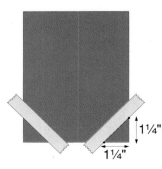

1¼"

1¼"

•With right sides together, fold the corner to a point, aligning the marks and the tape. Stitch next to the tape but not through it, forming the miter.

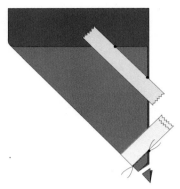

•To eliminate bulk, trim the seam ¼" to ⅜" from the stitching. Repeat for the second corner.

2. Turn the pocket right side out. Press the seam allowances to the wrong side.

3. Fuse interfacing to the pocket hem allowance.

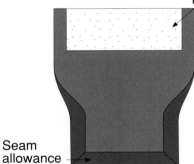

Interfacing

Seam allowance

4. Fold the pocket hem to the right side along the hemline. Stitch the hem's side seams, using a ⅝" seam allowance.

•Press the seams flat and then press them open.

•To reduce bulk, grade the seams and trim the corners at an angle.

•Turn the pocket right side out and press.

Timesaving Notions

I prefer using Sewer's Fix-It Tape as a stitching guide when sewing mitered corners. It is softer than household tape and can be repositioned several times without losing its stickiness.

Timesaving Notions

I like to use a Point Presser to quickly press the seam allowance open at the corners. This hardwood tool has a narrow (1"-wide) pressing surface that tapers to a point. Simply place the pocket seam over the pointed end of the Point Presser and press.

Timesaving Notions

Wonder-Under is a fusible-transfer web— a heat-sensitive adhesive applied to a removable paper backing. It is used for appliqués, fabric crafting, and fusing two fabrics together. Narrow strips of Wonder-Under are a real time-saver when positioning pockets and fusing hemlines. Other brands to look for are Fusible Film and Heat N Bond. Similar products available without the paper backing include Stitch Witchery, Fine Fuse, Transfer-Web, and Magic Fuse.

Timesaving Notions

The blind-hem foot is included in most sewing machine accessory boxes. Although designed for machine blindhemming, it also works well for edgestitching—the adjustable arm serves as a handy stitching guide.

5. Apply the pocket to the garment.

•To "baste" the pocket into position, use narrow strips of fusible-transfer web like Wonder-Under. Lightly fusing the pocket in place eliminates the need to stitch over pins that may cause dimples in the topstitched seam.

•Cut ¼"-wide strips of Wonder-Under or cut the ½" precut strips down the middle. (Use your rotary cutter and mat to make the job easy.)

•Position the strips on the pocket seam allowances as shown, about ¼" to ⅜" inside the pocket-edge fold. (The web side of the Wonder-Under should be next to the fabric, with the paper side up.) Following directions on the package, press the web in place and then peel off the paper backing.

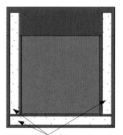

Wonder-Under

•Place the pocket on the garment. Cover the pocket with a press cloth and press to fuse-baste the pocket to the garment.

6. Replace the standard presser foot with a blindhem foot. Edgestitch the pocket to the garment.

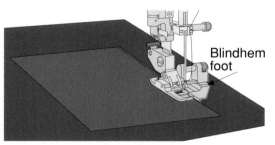

Blindhem foot

On the right side of the pocket, edgestitch close to the side and bottom of the pocket. Use the fold along the edge as a guide for the blindhem foot.

Double-Welt Pockets

Double-welt pockets are the trademark of a prestigious jacket. Making them takes a little longer than sewing patch pockets, but the sophisticated, polished look is certainly worth the extra time. It's easier than you'd imagine—just think of double-welt pockets

as large bound buttonholes. The pocket flap is optional. Try these shortcuts and make perfect pockets every time!

1. Stitch the pocket window.

•Transfer the pocket placement dots from the pattern to the right side of the jacket. Mark the corresponding dots on the wrong side of the pocket-lining pieces.

•With the right side of the pocket lining against the right side of the jacket, match the placement dots. Pin.

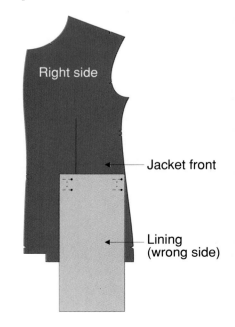

Right side

Jacket front

Lining (wrong side)

•Set the machine stitch length at 15 to
20 stitches per inch.
•Lower the sewing machine needle at
one end of the welt opening.
•Stitch around the opening, stitching
through the paper pattern and pivoting
exactly at the corners. The stitches perforate
the photocopied pattern, so that it's easy to
remove the paper after completing the
stitching.

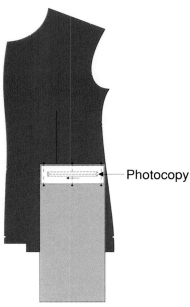

2. Clip through the center of the window,
cutting to within ¼" of the corner; then
carefully snip into the points. For reinforcement, restitch the opening after cutting.

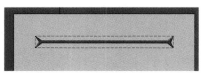

3. Press one side of the lining toward the
center of the opening, over the seam allowance. Understitch the lengthwise edges
of the window.

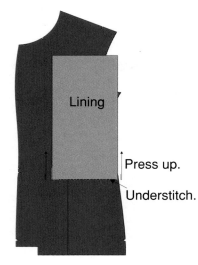

Repeat for the other side of the lining.

4. Turn the pocket lining to the wrong
side of the jacket and press. Now you have
a "window" in the jacket front.

5. Prepare the welt.
•Cut two strips for the welt from the
garment fabric. Cut each strip 2" longer than
the pocket window and 2" wide.

• With right sides together, machine-baste the strips together down the center.

Wrong side

• Refold the strips so that the right sides are exposed and the basted seam is in the center. Press.

Right side

6. Position the welts under the window and fuse-baste them in place.

• Using narrow strips of Wonder-Under, place the fusible side of the strips on the *wrong* side of the jacket, along the two long sides of the window.

• Press to fuse. Remove the paper backing from the strips.

Right side

7. Stitch the welts in place.

• Fold back the jacket front, exposing the original stitching for the pocket window.

• To secure the welt, restitch along the original stitching line. Stitch one long edge; then refold and stitch the other long edge. Repeat to stitch each short end.

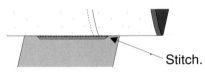

Stitch.

• Grade the welt seam allowances and the window seam allowances to reduce bulk.

• Remove the basting from the center of the welt.

8. Finish the pocket.

• If the pocket does not have a flap, fold up the lining section so that the lower edge meets the upper edge. Pin.

• Fold back the jacket front to expose the original seam. Restitch along the seam line to join the upper edges of the lining.

Restitch.

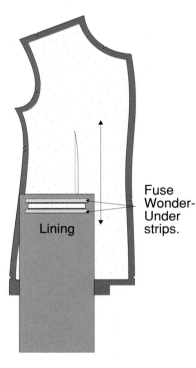

Fuse Wonder-Under strips.

Lining

• Place the welt on an appliqué pressing sheet on your ironing board. Position the jacket window, right side up, over the right side of the welt, centering the basted seam in the window's opening.

• When the welt is positioned exactly as desired, cover it with a press cloth and press to fuse the welt temporarily to the jacket.

• Stitch the pocket-lining side seams.

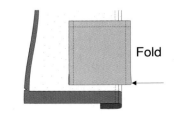

Fold

Flaps for the Double-Welt Pockets

For a truly professional tailored touch, add pocket flaps to your double-welt pockets.

1. Follow Steps 1 through 4 for the double-welt pocket.

> ### Note from Nancy
> *The pocket flap must fit exactly inside the welt opening. Without a stitching guide, it is easy to make the flap ¼" too big or too small. Making a photocopy of the flap pattern gives you precisely the correct size—it's the perfect stitching guide!*

2. Place the pocket-flap pieces with right sides together.

• Align the photocopy over the flap pieces and pin. Stitch, following the pattern's stitching lines.

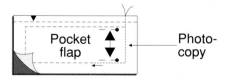

• If your pocket flap has rounded corners, use a slightly shorter stitch length when stitching the curved areas to achieve perfectly rounded corners.

• Remove the paper. Grade the seams and turn the pocket flap right side out. If desired, topstitch the pocket flap.

3. Slip the completed pocket flap into the opening between the pocket welts; pin.

Pocket welts
Pocket flap

• Fold back the jacket to expose the original window seam.

• Restitch along the seam line to secure the flap.

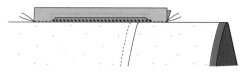

• Follow Step 8 for the double-welt pocket to finish the pocket.

Shoulder and Side Seams

Stitch the shoulder and side seams of the outer jacket. Press the seams flat and then press them open.

Sleeve Vents

Sleeve vents are common features of two-piece sleeves. The usual construction methods leave multiple layers of the fabric in the upper and lower vents, producing a bulky closure at the wrist. In addition, the edge of the lower layer of the vent is traditionally left unfinished.

Here's a way to solve both of these common problems: eliminate the bulk from the upper vent by mitering the corner, and neatly finish the under vent.

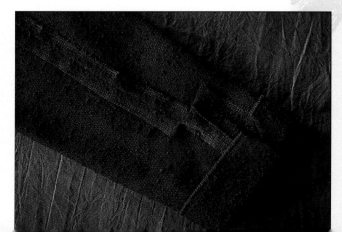

1. Stitch the side seam, joining the two parts of the sleeve.

2. Miter the corner on the upper vent.

• Fold the vent to the inside along the fold line. Fold the hem up to the correct length; pin.

• Using tiny clips or pins, mark the point at which the raw edges of the hem and the vent intersect. Unfold the fabric.

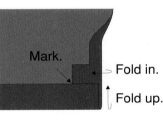

Upper sleeve

Mark.

Fold in.

Fold up.

• On the wrong side of the fabric, place tape between the marks. Extend the tape beyond the cut edges of the fabric.

• Fold the sleeve with right sides together, matching the marks and the ends of the tape.

3. Stitch, following the edge of the tape, to ensure an even miter.

• Trim the seam allowances to ¼".

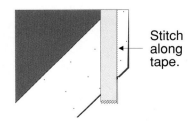

Stitch along tape.

• Press the seam open.

• Turn the miter right side out. Press.

4. Finish the edge of the lower vent.

• With right sides together, fold up the hemline.

• Stitch a ¼" seam along the edge of the vent.

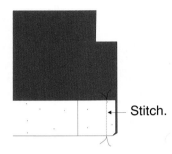

Stitch.

• Press the seam flat and then press it open over the point presser.

• Turn the seam right side out.

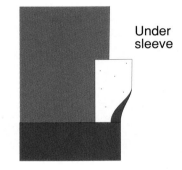

Under sleeve

Setting In the Sleeves

Most patterns instruct you to sew two rows of gathering stitches and then to pull up the bobbin threads to ease the sleeve cap. Here's a quicker method to ease sleeve caps—the "finger easing" technique.

1. Set your sewing machine for a straight stitch. If the machine has a dual feed, disengage it.

> ### Note from Nancy
> *For most fabrics, set the machine for a normal stitch length (10 to 12 stitches per inch). The length of the stitch varies with the weight of the fabric: use a longer stitch length for heavier fabrics and a shorter stitch length for lightweight fabrics.*

2. Finger-ease the upper edge of the sleeve.

• Lower the needle into the fabric ½" from the edge of the sleeve. Press your finger firmly against the back of the presser foot.

Timesaving Notions
To quickly press mitered corners, use a Point Presser. The wood of the Point Presser absorbs moisture, preventing the possibility of creating shine on the fabric.

• Begin sewing along the upper edge of the sleeve, trying to stop the fabric from flowing through the machine smoothly. The fabric will begin to bunch up between your finger and the presser foot.

• Stitch 2" to 3" and then remove your finger, releasing the bunched-up fabric. Repeat the process to finger-ease the entire sleeve cap.

> **Note from Nancy**
> *Finger easing will not completely prevent the fabric from flowing behind the presser foot. However, it does cause the feed dogs to ease each stitch slightly.*

3. Pin the sleeve to the armhole, matching notches and underarm seams and aligning the large dot on the sleeve cap to the shoulder seam. Stitch the entire armhole, using a ⅝" seam allowance.

4. Stitch the underarm area (notch to notch) a second time, using a ⅜" seam allowance. Trim the underarm seam allowance to the second row of stitching, leaving the sleeve-cap allowances ⅝" wide.

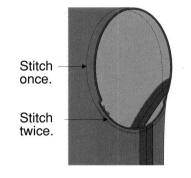

Stitch once.

Stitch twice.

5. Place the sleeve on a tailor's ham so that the sleeve allowances extend toward

the sleeve cap. Press from the wrong side, using the tip of the iron and pressing just ⅛" beyond the seam line to prevent flattening the cap. These pressing steps retain the sleeve's rounded shape.

> **Note from Nancy**
> *Never press a sleeve from the right side—the weight of the iron will flatten the roll of the sleeve.*

Sleeve Heads

To complete each jacket sleeve, insert a sleeve head. A sleeve head is a strip of polyester fleece (or, in traditional tailoring, lamb's wool) placed in the cap of the sleeve. It fills out the fullness of the cap and reduces wrinkles in the sleeve and shoulder line.

1. To make two sleeve heads, cut a piece of polyester fleece 3" by 20". Fold under 1" along one long edge.

2. Topstitch ½" from the fold. The sleeve head should now measure 2" by 20".

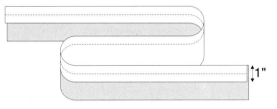

1"

3. Cut the strip in half so that each sleeve head measures 2" by 10".

4. Center the sleeve head in the cap of the sleeve.

5. Align the folded edge of the sleeve head with the armhole/sleeve seam-allowance edges. The side with the 1"-wide fold faces the sleeve cap. Pin in place.

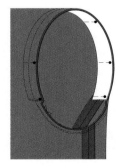

6. Secure the sleeve head by restitching the sleeve seam. Because the sleeve head is next to the sleeve, follow the original stitching line by restitching the seam from the other (jacket) side.

7. From the wrong side, press the finished sleeve over a ham, pressing all the seam allowances toward the sleeve.

Applying the Under Collar

The next step is to apply the under collar to the jacket unit. (Later the upper collar will be attached to the lining unit, using the same steps and techniques.) Remember— the under collar is applied to the jacket unit and the upper collar to the lining unit.

1. Transfer the dot markings from the pattern to the collar at the center back, shoulder seams, and lapel points. Mark as accurately as possible with a marking pen or pencil. Transfer the corresponding dot markings from the pattern pieces to the jacket at the center back, shoulder seams, and lapel points.

2. Pin the under collar to the neckline. Match the shoulder seams, center back, and especially the lapel-point markings as precisely as possible.

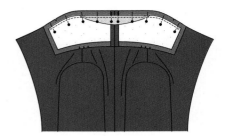

3. Stitch the under collar to the jacket unit.

•Ease the two uneven fabric lengths together by stitching with the jacket side up and the longer collar layer down, next to the feed dogs.

> ### Note from Nancy
> *You can apply this simple easing principle—placing the longer layer down, next to the feed dogs—to most situations you will encounter in sewing. For example, try this technique when seaming the back shoulder to the shorter front shoulder of a garment or when setting in sleeve caps that require easing. I guarantee you'll find countless ways to sew better and faster by utilizing this simple technique.*

•Begin and end the line of stitching at the lapel points. Stitch in place (set your stitch length to 0 stitches per inch) to lock the beginning and end of the seam.

4. Intermittently clip both the neckline and collar seam allowances to the stitching line. The first and last clips should be at the lapel points.

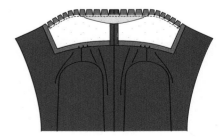

5. After clipping, reinforce the seam by restitching the neckline/collar seam. (The seam can be weakened during clipping.)

6. Press the neckline/collar seam open. Because this is a curved seam, press it over a curved surface such as a pressing ham. Do not trim the neckline seam allowances at this time.

Assembling the Lining Unit

Here are some possible sewing units for the lining unit:

- Darts
- Lining back
- Lining front
- Upper collar
- Sleeves

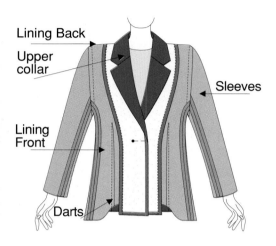

Lining Back

Upper collar

Sleeves

Lining Front

Darts

Lining Back

1. Machine-baste the center back pleat. Press the pleat to the left side. At the top and waistline of the pleat, machine-stitch through all the layers, using a decorative stitch.

> #### Note from Nancy
> Most back linings have a center back pleat. Usually, the pattern guide sheet instructs you to cross-stitch the pleat in place by hand, at the top and waistline of the pleat. Experience has shown me that this handwork isn't as durable as I like. Try using one of your machine's decorative stitches instead. The machine stitches are attractive, faster, and more secure!

2. Stitch the back neckline facing to the lining.

- Pin the back neck facing (an outward curve) to the neck lining (an inward curve).

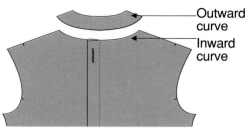

Outward curve

Inward curve

- Stitch the seam with the back neck facing down, next to the feed dogs, so that the longer layer will automatically be eased.

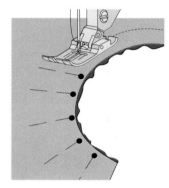

3. Press and clip the seam.

Lining Front

1. Prepare the hems on the lining pieces.

- Press up the hems on the front lining pieces.
- Pin the lining to the jacket facing. Fold up the hem of the lining so that the lining hem is 1" shorter than the jacket facing hemline.

Fold up lining hem.

• Press up the lining hem.

Note from Nancy

In the past, it's been a challenge to achieve a neat, flat finish where the lining and the facing meet the jacket hem. Pressing up the lining hem BEFORE stitching it to the facing solves the problem and streamlines the process.

2. Stitch the front facing to the front lining.

• The front lining is an outward curve and the front facing is an inward curve. Sew the two together with the lining down, next to the feed dogs, so that it will automatically ease.

• Press the seam flat. Press the seam allowance toward the lining.

3. Sew the front and back lining pieces together at the shoulder and underarm seams. Press the seam allowances flat and then press them open.

Note from Nancy

If you have a machine that includes decorative stitches, you can personalize your jacket by adding decorative stitching to the seam that joins the facing to the lining.

I like to monogram the pattern number and "Made by" in the stitching.

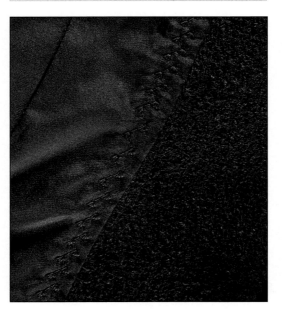

Setting In the Lining Sleeves

Follow the guidelines listed under "Setting In the Sleeves" on page 98.

Applying the Upper Collar

Refer to "Applying the Under Collar" on page 100 and follow the same steps to attach the upper collar to the lining unit.

Shoulder Pads

Before stitching the jacket and lining units together, add shoulder pads to the jacket unit.

1. Align the straight edge of the shoulder pad with the edges of the sleeve/armhole seam allowance. Center the pad over the shoulder seam.

Pin the pad in place from the right side. In the same way, pin the other shoulder pad in place.

2. Try on the jacket. Reposition the shoulder pads, if necessary.

3. Tack one shoulder pad to the armhole/shoulder seam allowance.

• When attaching the shoulder pad by hand, sew a tack with a "shank," like you do when sewing on a button.

• When attaching the shoulder pad by machine, use a fringe or tailor tack foot.

Note from Nancy

Shanks won't compress the pad—they allow the pad to move slightly, preventing pulling and puckering on the right side of the jacket.

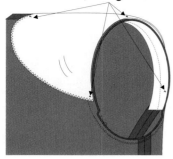

Tack, using a shank.

4. Tack the remaining shoulder pad to the armhole/shoulder seam allowance.

Sewing the Jacket and Lining Units Together

1. Align the jacket and lining units with right sides together.

•Match the neckline seams. Make certain that the lapel point dot of the upper collar aligns exactly with the lapel point dot on the under collar. Other crucial areas to match are the shoulder seams and center back seams of the collar.

•Periodically pin the two neckline seams together to prevent shifting while sewing the lapel area.

•Pin the collar and lapel edges together.

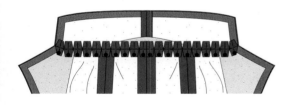

2. Machine-baste the collar and lapel edges together.

•Baste the collar seam from the edges to the lapel dot. Do not catch any neckline seam allowances in the seam line.

•Baste the lapel seam, starting and ending at the lapel dots. Again, do not catch any neckline seam allowances in the seam line.

•Finger-press the seams open. Turn the fabric right side out. Check the lapel points: the seam lines should meet exactly at the dots.

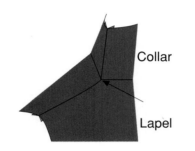

Collar

Lapel

•If the seam lines meet at the lapel-point dots, you can restitch the two seams, using 12 to 15 stitches per inch. If not, remove the basting stitches and try again!

3. Press the seams flat and then press them open. Grade the seam allowances to minimize bulk.

4. Stitch the top edge of the collar. Wrap the upper collar seam allowance to the under collar side, positioning the stitching line along the fold.

•Pin the unsewn edges of the collars together. The under collar is slightly smaller than the upper collar. Stitch with the upper collar down, next to the feed dogs. For a more durable seam, adjust for a shorter stitch length—approximately 18 stitches per inch.

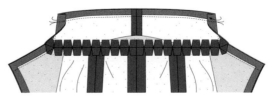

•Press the collar seam just completed. Grade the under-collar seam allowance to ¼" and the upper-collar seam allowance to ⅜".

•Trim the excess bulk from the point of the collar. If the fabric ravels easily, seal the seam edges with Fray Check.

Timesaving Notions
The fringe or tailor tack foot is usually included in your machine's accessory box, or it can be purchased separately. Set the machine at the widest bar-tack setting. As the thread sews over the high center bar of the foot, a shank is created.

Timesaving Notions
To seal seam edges, use a liquid sealant such as Fray Check, No-Fray, or Stop-Fray. It dries clear and is completely washable and dry-cleanable. You can also lock ends of serged stitching with a drop of Fray Check. Apply one or two drops at the seam ends and allow to dry.

103

•Trim only the collar seam allowances of both units (that are pressed toward the collar) as shown. Both neckline seam allowances (that are pressed toward the jacket) must be left at ⅝" width.

5. Turn the collar right side out. Pin the upper and lower collars together along the neckline seams, inserting pins in the ditch formed by the seams.

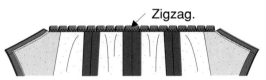

6. Turn the neckline/collar seams to the wrong side.
•Pin the seam allowances of the two necklines together.
•Zigzag the two seam allowances together, removing the pins as you stitch.

7. Stitch the facing to the jacket front.
•With right sides together and matching the roll-line clip marks, pin the front facing to the jacket front.
•Wrap the neckline seam allowance as shown.

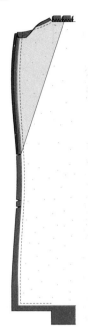

•Between the waistline and the neckline, the front facing will be longer than the jacket front. To automatically ease the layers, sew with the jacket next to the foot and the front facing next to the feed dogs.
•Press the center front seam flat and then press it open.

•Grade the seam allowances. Clip the allowances to the stitching line at the roll-line marking, as shown.

•Above the roll-line marking, grade the facing seam allowance to ⅜" and the jacket front allowance to ¼".
•Below the roll-line marking, grade the facing seam allowance to ¼" and the jacket front allowance to ⅜". Turn jacket right side out.

8. Working from the right side of the jacket, align the lapel and collar seam lines. This alignment will be easy because the seam lines were pressed during construction. Using a press cloth, press from the right side.

Fast, Professional Finishing Techniques

To finish the jacket, secure the units together. This will prevent the lining from shifting when the jacket is put on and taken off.

1. Join the jacket and lining at the underarm seam.
•Align the underarm seam of the lining with the underarm seam of the jacket. Pin the two sleeves together for a distance of 3" (1½" on each side of the underarm seam).
•With the jacket side up, stitch in-the-ditch 1½" on each side of the underarm seam.

Stitch in-the-ditch.

1½"   1½"

2. Align the shoulder seams at the sleeve caps. The shoulder pad will be between the two units. Hand-tack the layers together at the shoulder seams.

Tack together.

Hemming the Jacket and Lining Units

1. Press up the jacket hemline and loosely handstitch the hem.

2. Press up the lining hemline.

3. Try on the jacket. Have someone help you smooth the jacket and pin through to the lining at the waistline. Also pin through to the sleeve lining, right above the elbow and around the full circumference of the sleeve. Take off the jacket.

4. Temporarily pin a ½" tuck in the lining pieces, below the waistline pins and below the elbow pins. Taper the waistline tuck to the front facing where there is no excess fabric.

Pin the lining hemline to the jacket hem, about 1" up from the jacket hemline. Repeat for the sleeve linings.

5. Hand-blindstitch the lining hem to the jacket hem, catching only the folded edge of the lining. (The stitches should not be exposed.) Repeat for the sleeve lining hems.

6. Remove all the pins, including those holding the ½" tucks. Smooth the excess fabric (created by the tucks) toward the hemline.

Note from Nancy
The excess lining length will allow unrestricted movement and prevent pulling on the right side of the jacket.

Topstitching Tips

One of the final details in sewing a jacket is topstitching around the lapel and collar. Although this stitching is certainly optional, it adds another custom accent and enhances the stability of the edges. The key is to topstitch distinctively and evenly.

1. Change to a topstitching needle.

2. Wind two threads in the bobbin. The two threads can be wound onto the bobbin simultaneously.

Note from Nancy
When using two threads through the needle for topstitching, it's also important to use two threads in the bobbin. The stitch will be reversible and more durable. Plus, you won't have to worry about differences in the top and bottom of the stitch as you pass the lapel roll line.

Timesaving Notions
A topstitching needle, available only in size 90, has a wider, longer eye than a traditional needle. It can easily accommodate the two strands of sewing machine thread used for topstitching.

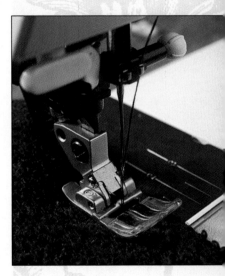

3. Lengthen the stitch length slightly, to about eight stitches per inch.

- Adjust the needle and the bobbin tensions.
- Thread the two top-thread strands through the machine as if you were threading with one strand.
- Thread the bobbin case as if you were threading with one strand.

4. Stitch from the bottom hem edge to the lapel. If possible, stop with the needle in the down position, a few inches below the point where the lapel and collar meet. Place a pin on the lapel even with and parallel to the edge of the collar.

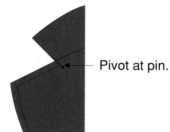

Pivot at pin.

5. Topstitch to the pin and stop with the needle in the fabric.

6. Pivot and sew along the pin to the point where the collar joins the lapel, counting the number of stitches. Stop with the needle in the well of the seam.

Pivot again at seam line.

7. Pivot and sew the same number of stitches in the well of the collar seam; stop with the needle in the fabric.

8. Pivot and continue to topstitch around the collar.

Topstitch collar.

9. Repeat the process (in reverse) for the other end of the collar and the other lapel.

Buttonholes

Many sewing machines offer fully automated buttonhole stitches. Some of them, such as the keyhole, are designed specifically for jackets and coats.

Whichever buttonhole you choose, be sure to practice on an interfaced piece of your jacket fabric before stitching on the actual jacket.

> ### Note from Nancy
> The method I use most is a corded buttonhole. The cording used in this quick-to-sew, professional-looking buttonhole prevents the hole from stretching out of shape. I find that I get the best thread match for the cording by zigzagging over six strands of thread.

1. Loop the cording over the extra toe of your buttonhole foot. (Some will have this toe in the front; others in the back.) Place the cord's looped end toward the center of the jacket.

2. Sew the buttonhole, stitching over the cording while holding the cording taut.

3. After the buttonhole is sewn, pull the extra tails of the cording tight.

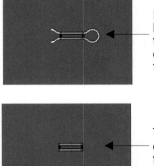

Place loop toward center front.

Trim cording tails.

•Trim the tails next to the buttonhole.
•Flatten and press the buttonhole. The cording ends will automatically withdraw and be hidden in the stitches.

Buttons

Use your sewing machine's fringe or tailor tack foot to sew on buttons. The high center bar of the foot helps create the button's shank.

1. Position your button on the jacket with transparent tape.

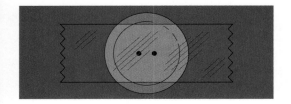

2. Set your machine in the left needle position for bar tacking ("0" stitch length, wide zigzag). Turn the wheel by hand to sew the first stitches, in order to check the correct width of the zigzag for your buttons.

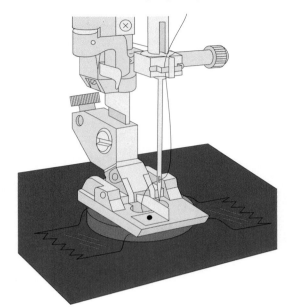

3. Zigzag five or six times. Lock the stitches by setting your stitch width to "0" and stitching several times in the left needle position. Cut your thread, leaving 10" to 12" thread tails.

4. Stitch the remaining buttons in the same manner and remove the transparent tape.

5. Pull the buttons up so that the excess threads forming the shank lie between the buttons and the fabric.

6. Pull the long thread tails through the buttons and the fabric so that they meet at the shank.

•Thread the tails on a needle. To form the thread shank under the button, tightly wrap the thread around the shank a few times.

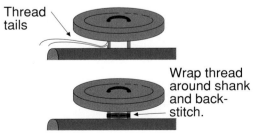

Thread tails

Wrap thread around shank and back-stitch.

•Backstitch several times into the shank to fasten the thread tails. Seal the knot with Fray Check.

Designer TOUCHES

Press, cut, peel, fuse, stitch! These are the five steps to applying a basic appliqué with the use of a paper-backed fusible web. But there's more—much more—to appliqué. I've devoted the greatest part of this chapter to appliqués—from basic to creative variations. Make a garment from a simple pattern or choose a ready-made garment with simple styling and add an appliqué. You'll be amazed how quickly and easily you can create one-of-a-kind

![Pocket watch illustration]

Timesaving Notions
To provide support and stability, I like to back my knits with an interfacing like Pellon's Knit Shape fusible interfacing. This prevents bagging and sagging of the appliqué after the garment has been washed several times.

The Basics of Appliqué

Choosing Appliqué Fabrics

The key to successful appliqué is fabric choice. Check your scrap box for appliqué fabric possibilities or purchase a specific fabric for your embellishment. In either case, usually a small amount of fabric is all that is needed. Consider compatibility—whether the appliqué fabrics have similar washing and drying requirements as the fashion fabric. Then continue the selection process, choosing components that have color, texture, shading, design, or fiber contents that give you the look that you need. Here are some fabric possibilities for appliqués:

• **Woven fabrics,** such as calico, pindots, solids, pillow ticking, polyester/cotton blends, polished cotton or chintz, white-on-white textured fabrics, and denim are popular fabrics to use for appliqués. In addition to using pieces of plain or patterned fabrics, consider cutting around a larger printed design and using that design as an appliqué. Sections of recycled garments, especially denim, can also provide interesting details.

• **Knit fabrics,** including velour, interlock knits, quilted interlock knits, and sweatshirt fleece, add unique interest to appliqués. Get two looks from one fabric by using both the right and wrong sides.

• **Specialty fabrics** with a nap, such as washed wool, lace, Ultrasuede, corduroy, satin, terry cloth, velvet, and velour are interesting selections for appliqués. Experiment by running the nap in different directions.

Preparing Fabric for Appliqué

Always pretreat the fabrics that will be used for an appliqué. Wash and dry them as you plan to care for the appliquéd garment.

Use a fusible knit interfacing to stabilize knit fabrics that will be used for the appliqué. Fuse the interfacing to the back of the knit before cutting out the appliqué design. Woven fabrics that ravel excessively can also be backed with interfacing to minimize raveling.

Using Fusible Web

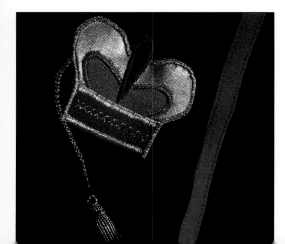

Although there are many ways to add an appliqué to a garment, using a fusible web is one of the easiest and most versatile. You'll be amazed at how simple it is!

1. Trace the appliqué design onto the paper side of a paper-backed fusible web such as Wonder-Under. There may be several sections to a design, so be sure to trace each part individually.

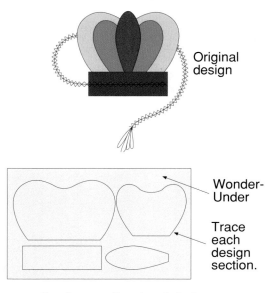

Original design

Wonder-Under

Trace each design section.

• Simple, nondirectional designs can be traced with pen, pencil, or marking pen.

• Designs that have a definite right and left, or those that contain words, will produce a mirror image if traced directly onto the Wonder-Under. Use a product such as the Fabric Pattern Transfer Kit to reverse the design for tracing.

Reverse design and trace.

Timesaving Notions

Use an Easy Way Appliqué Pressing Sheet to preassemble the design. This nonstick pressing sheet allows you to fuse various parts of a design together and then position and fuse the entire appliqué to the garment. The pressing sheet is transparent, allowing you to easily see where portions of the appliqué are placed. The sheet can be used over and over. Using it is almost effortless!

• For more detailed designs that have several parts, determine where the various design components will overlap. Extend the cut edges of the lower layer by ⅛". The ⅛" extension ensures that the base fabric won't peek through after the appliqué is finished.

• Number the pieces in the order in which they will be joined, working from the bottom toward the top.

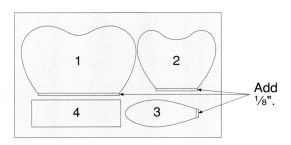

Add ⅛".

2. Roughly cut out the traced Wonder-Under appliqué design.

3. Using a hot, dry iron, press the Wonder-Under to the wrong side of the appliqué fabric for three seconds and let the fabric cool.

4. Cut out the appliqué design, following the pattern outlines.

5. Peel off the paper backing, and the appliqué is ready to use!

6. If you are working with a detailed design made up of several parts, assemble the design before fusing it to the garment to ensure accurate positioning of the various appliqué sections.

• Position the individual fused appliqué pieces on one half of the pressing sheet, beginning with the piece that is on the bottom or appears farthest away. Make sure underneath areas have ⅛" extensions added so that the upper pieces can be easily overlapped.

• Continue placing pieces on the pressing sheet, working upward and overlapping ⅛" where sections meet. Repeat until the design is completed, placing the top pieces last.

• Cover the layered appliqué with the remaining portion of the pressing sheet. Press for five to 10 seconds, using a dry iron set to "wool." Allow the pressing sheet to cool. Remove the fused appliqué, peeling away the pressing sheet. The Wonder-Under will adhere to the fabric but not to the pressing sheet.

7. Transfer any appliqué detail markings onto the right side of the fusible appliqué with a washable marking pen.

8. Before you fuse the appliqué to the garment, it's important to check its position. If you're adding an appliqué to a purchased garment, try on the garment. Place the wrong side of the appliqué on the right side of the garment. Move the appliqué until you're satisfied with its placement. If you're adding the appliqué to a garment you're sewing, stitch or pin the shoulder seams together. Try on the garment and then position the appliqué as desired.

9. To fuse the appliqué to the garment:

• Cover the positioned appliqué with a damp press cloth.

• Fuse for 10 seconds with an iron set at "wool."

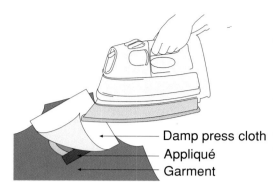

Damp press cloth
Appliqué
Garment

• For large appliqués, lift and reposition the iron after fusing the first section, overlapping the original area. Fuse for another 10 seconds. Repeat until entire design is fused.

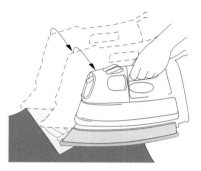

Finishing the Edges of the Appliqué

Setting Up Your Machine for Satin Stitching

Although the appliqué is secured to the garment by fusing, adding a row of satin stitching around its edges will make the appliqué permanent and more attractive. After the appliqué is positioned and fused, it's time to satin-stitch.

1. Replace the conventional presser foot with the open toe or appliqué foot.

2. Loosen the upper tension by two numbers or notches and test the stitch on a scrap to determine the best setting for your machine. Loosening the tension draws the top thread slightly to the wrong side of the fabric and prevents the bobbin thread from showing on the right side of the garment.

3. In the needle, use rayon or cotton machine embroidery thread for a lustrous appearance or metallic threads for a glistening accent. Use a lightweight thread in the bobbin.

4. Insert a new machine needle. It's an inexpensive way to prevent fabric snags and to produce smoother, more uniform stitches.

• Use a size 70 (11 American) or 80 (12 American) needle with machine embroidery thread.

• For metallic threads, use a larger-eyed needle, size 90/14, to prevent the thread fibers from splitting.

5. Set the machine for a zigzag stitch of narrow to medium width and short satin-stitch length.

Note from Nancy
In most cases, smaller appliqué pieces require narrower zigzag stitches. The stitch length varies somewhat depending on the fabric and the desired look. It is helpful to make a sample of the various stitch widths available on your machine. This will give you an idea of how the different settings look and will help determine the most appropriate settings for various portions of the appliqué.

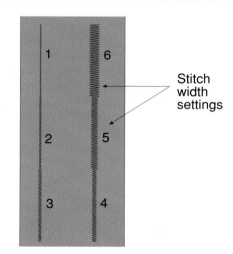

Stitch width settings

6. If possible, set the machine so that the needle stops in the "down" position. This keeps your last stitch positioned under your presser foot and makes it easier to pivot the fabric and make precise corners.

Satin-Stitching Techniques

Practice on a sample of fabric before stitching on the actual appliqué. You'll perfect your technique and the finished appliqué will look more professional.

General Stitching Guidelines

1. Use a temporary stabilizer such as Wash-Away or Stitch-N-Tear on the wrong side of the fabric to support it and promote even stitching. After stitching is completed, the backing is removed.

Timesaving Notions
Lingerie/Bobbin Thread, made of nylon, is the perfect bobbin thread for appliqué stitching and charted needlework. It is strong yet lightweight and will not add bulk to the wrong side of the fabric.

Timesaving Notions
Metallic threads are more brittle than cotton or rayon threads and tend to split or fray while sewing. Sewers Aid, a liquid coating, helps remedy this problem. Before sewing, apply a line of Sewers Aid along the length of the spool. The liquid lightly coats the thread as it unwinds, preventing splitting and fraying. Frequently reapply a line of Sewers Aid to the spool of metallic thread during the appliqué process.

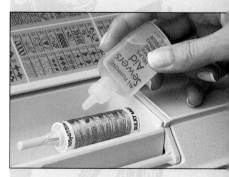

113

2. Place the larger portion of the appliqué design to the left of the machine to allow for greater fabric maneuverability. As you stitch, the left "zig" should catch the appliqué and the right "zag" should be on the garment—just past the raw edge of the appliqué. (The raw edges of the appliqué should be completely covered by the stitches.)

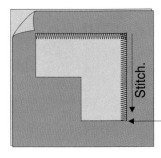

Stop with needle in right position.

Stitching Inside Corners

1. Stitch to the corner; then continue stitching three to four stitches (as far as the width of the zigzag stitch) past the corner.

2. Stop with the needle in the left "zig" position, with the needle down in the fabric.

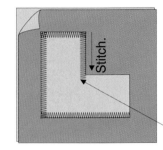

Stitch.

Stop with needle in left position.

3. For detailed designs that include several colors and fabric pieces, begin by stitching the background (underneath) sections in place and ending with the foreground. This gives the appliqué dimension and provides greater realism.

3. Raise the presser foot and pivot the fabric so that the next side is in line with the needle.

4. Lower the presser foot and continue stitching.

Stitching Outside Corners

1. Stitch to the corner of the design, with the final stitch in the garment just past the corner of the appliqué.

2. Stop with the needle in the right "zag" position. The needle should remain down in the fabric.

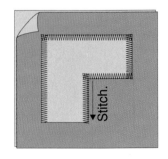

Stitch.

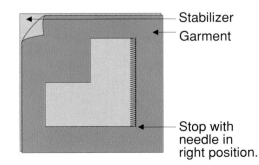

Stabilizer

Garment

Stop with needle in right position.

3. Raise the presser foot and pivot the fabric so that the next side of the appliqué is in line with the needle.

4. Lower the presser foot and continue stitching.

Stitching Curves

1. Using your left index finger, anchor the fabric to the bed of the sewing machine.

2. Use your left hand to turn and control the fabric's movement. Gently turn the fabric as you stitch, allowing the fabric to gradually pivot and produce a smooth, even curve.

3. On sharp curves, it may be necessary to raise the presser foot periodically to achieve a smooth curve. Stop with the needle in the right "zag" position. Raise the presser foot and slightly pivot the fabric. Lower the presser foot and continue stitching.

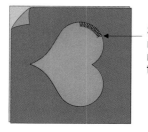

Stop with needle in right position; pivot.

Stitching Scallops

1. Mark the fabric at the center of the scallop's point. This will indicate where to begin pivoting.

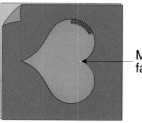

Mark fabric.

2. Hold the fabric taut as you satin-stitch around the curve of the scallop. Gently guide the fabric around the curve, pivoting gradually and often to make a smooth curve. If it is necessary to raise the presser foot to pivot, stop with the needle down in the fabric and in the right "zag" of the zigzag stitch. Then raise the presser foot to pivot.

3. When you reach the mark made in Step 1, stop with the needle down in the fabric and in the left "zig" of the zigzag stitch.

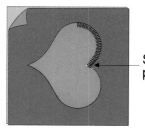

Stop and pivot.

4. Lift the presser foot and pivot the fabric as necessary to continue stitching around the next scallop.

5. Lower the presser foot and continue stitching.

Stitching Points

1. Stitch the first side of the appliqué. As you approach the point, gradually decrease the stitch width, working to a straight stitch at the point. Stop at the point, with the needle down in the fabric.

Decrease stitch width.

2. Raise the presser foot. Pivot the fabric until the next side of the appliqué is lined up with the presser foot.

3. Lower the presser foot and resume stitching, gradually increasing the stitch width to the original setting.

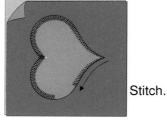

Stitch.

Stitching Triangles

1. Satin-stitch the first side of the triangle.
2. Near the point, stitch until the left "zig" of the zigzag stitch puts the needle off the fabric and on the other side of the point. Stop with the needle down in the fabric.

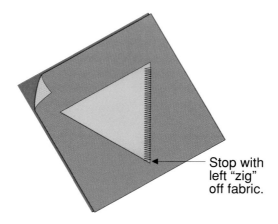

Stop with left "zig" off fabric.

3. Raise the presser foot and pivot the fabric until the point of the triangle is facing you. The point should be lined up between the toes of the presser foot. (The fabric needs to be moved only slightly.)

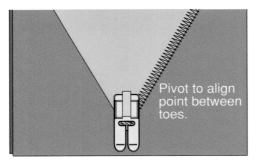

Pivot to align point between toes.

4. Continue stitching to the point, gradually decreasing the stitch width to "0" at the point.

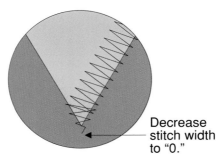

Decrease stitch width to "0."

5. Stop with the needle in the fabric at the point, pivot the fabric 180°, and begin stitching the other side, gradually increasing the stitch width from "0" to a medium stitch width.

6. When the zigzag stitch is at medium width, you may need to stop with the needle in the left "zig" of the zigzag and pivot the fabric to line the needle up correctly with the edge of the triangle.

Tying Off the Stitching

After the appliqué is stitched in place, set the stitch length at "0" and the stitch width at "0." Let the machine needle "dance" in place for several stitches to lock and secure the stitching.

Embellishing the Appliqué with Stitching

The inside of the appliqué design can be embellished with stitching to add dimensional effects and shading details. Here are some basic stitches to be used for inner details.

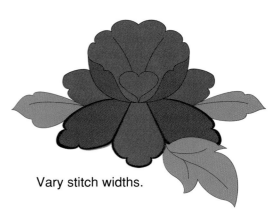

Vary stitch widths.

1. Straightstitch, using a short stitch length.

2. Use the satin stitch and vary the stitch width. Start with a wide stitch and gradually decrease the width to "0."

3. Couching gives a raised effect to the design. Lay a narrow ribbon or six strands of thread over the line to be stitched. Sew over the threads, using a zigzag stitch set at a stitch length a little longer than that used for normal satin stitching.

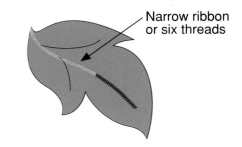

Narrow ribbon or six threads

4. To produce shading, use two colors of thread from the same color family. First, satin-stitch the line or edge, using a stitch with a slightly longer length than usual. Then add a second row of zigzag stitching, using the slightly longer stitch length, a different shade of thread than the first row, and slightly overlapping the stitching to blend the thread colors.

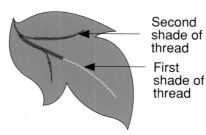

Second shade of thread

First shade of thread

5. Experiment with the decorative stitches on your sewing machine by decreasing the stitch length, narrowing the stitch width, or both. The feather stitch and blindhem stitch produce interesting effects when used in this manner.

1. Feather stitch

2. Feather stitch decreased

3. Blindhem stitch

4. Blindhem stitch decreased

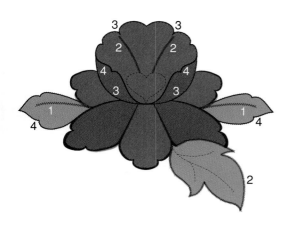

Beyond the Basics

Painted Appliqués

The *Sewing With Nancy* Challenge, a contest to commemorate 10 years of television programming, revealed the wide range of creative sewing being done by *Sewing With Nancy* viewers! Grand Prize Winner Virginia Martin of Staunton, Virginia, embellished an off-white pinafore with a cutwork hem and an entire carousel of appliquéd animals.

Virginia chose to paint her appliqué fabric to give the designs greater detail. After fusing the appliqués to the garment, she "painted" her designs with machine embroidery. Virginia's technique is unique and fun!

1. Fuse Wonder-Under to the wrong side of a rectangle of white cotton broadcloth cut slightly larger than the appliqué design.

2. Place the fabric over a photocopy of the design and hold them up to a sunny window. Trace the design, using a black or brown fine-point fabric marking pen.

3. Paint each section of the appliqué, using permanent fabric markers.

4. Cut out each appliqué, remove the paper backing, position on the garment, and fuse.

5. Satin-stitch the edges of the appliqué using machine embroidery threads. (See pages 113 through 116, "Finishing the Edges of the Appliqué," for machine setup and techniques.)

Timesaving Notions

Permanent designs can be created easily with Fashion Craft Permanent Fabric Markers. The brush-style nibs produce broad or fine lines, and the colors mix together beautifully. When set with a hot, dry iron, the colors are machine washable, fade-resistant, and non-toxic. The finished fabric will retain its natural softness and comfort. The 12-color set includes a selection of bright colors, plus black and gray.

6. Add detail to the appliqué with machine embroidery.
- Back the fabric with stabilizer.
- Adjust the machine for a zigzag satin stitch with a short stitch length.

- Use your left hand to guide the fabric through the machine. Use your right hand to adjust the stitch width dial as you stitch.
- Stitch the background areas first, working toward the foreground. This multilayer stitching adds texture and detail.

Layered Appliqué

Mary Reynolds of Surprise, Arizona, a *Sewing With Nancy* Challenge Second Place Winner, quilted a jacket with an original Southwest design. Through quilting and appliqué, Mary created a design representing Native American women and their pottery in a natural setting of mountains, desert, pueblos, and saguaro cactus.

Mary used two techniques to appliqué her jacket: For the small appliqués, she used the traditional paper-backed fusible web technique. For the larger appliqué pieces, she found that the fusible web made the fabric too stiff for quilting and decided to use fusible thread instead of web to position the pieces.

Her unique technique was also used to create the appliqués on this child's vest.

1. Cut out the larger background appliqué pieces.

2. Position the appliqué pieces in place on the garment and pin.

3. Insert ThreadFuse between the appliqué piece and the garment, a few inches at a time, very close to the outside edge of the appliqué. Fuse the appliqué in place with the tip of a hot, dry iron. This technique leaves the appliquéd section soft enough to quilt.

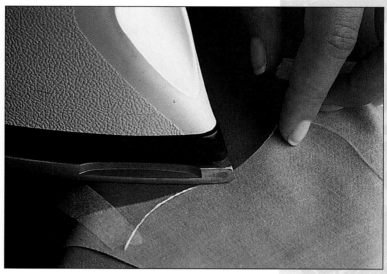

4. Fuse paper-backed fusible web to the backs of the small appliqué pieces.

5. Peel off the paper backing, position each piece on the vest, and fuse.

6. Satin-stitch around the edges of the appliqué.

7. After all the appliqué is finished, machine-quilt each section of the garment. Complete the garment, following the instructions on the pattern guide sheet.

Dimensional Appliqué

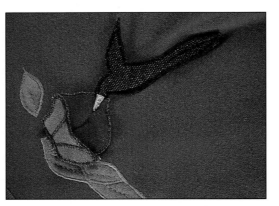

Appliqué provides so many options! Here's a variation that adds a layer of padding to provide extra dimension to portions of the design. Simply make a fabric "sandwich," satin-stitch only a portion of the appliqué design to the garment, and leave the remainder unattached.

Knits are a good fabric choice for this appliqué variation. Be sure to back the knit fabric with a fusible knit interfacing to keep the appliqué from stretching out of shape.

1. Draw the design on the paper side of Wonder-Under and fuse it onto the desired fabric. Cut the appliqué out of the fabric and peel off the paper backing.

2. Fuse a piece of Wonder-Under to another rectangle of the same fabric and peel off the paper backing. This will be the bottom layer.

3. Make a sandwich of the fabric layers with polyester fleece between.

• Place a piece of fleece against the Wonder-Under side of the bottom rectangle. Fuse together.

• Place the appliqué on the fleece, with the Wonder-Under toward the fleece. Fuse the appliqué to the fleece. The fabric sandwich now has three layers: the cutout design backed with Wonder-Under, fleece, and the bottom layer of fashion fabric backed with Wonder-Under.

• Cut around the design to trim the excess fleece and fabric.

Trim.

Cutout fabric appliqué backed with Wonder-Under

Fleece

Fabric fused to Wonder-Under

4. If there are any inner detail markings on the design, stitch the details at this time.

• Place the design on a piece of stabilizer that extends beyond the design.

• Stitch the inner details.

5. Satin-stitch around the outer edges.

• The "zig" should be stitched on the fabric and the "zag" off the edge of the fabric onto the stabilizer.

Stabilizer

• Gently tear away the stabilizer.

• Satin-stitch a second time around the design.

> ### Note from Nancy
> To give a design even more dimension, sew a double-pointed dart on the back. Fold the area to be shaped with right sides together. Create the dart by stitching from the center to each point.

6. Attach the piece to the garment by sewing only a portion of it to the garment, leaving the remainder unattached.

Stitch to garment.

Satin-stitch

Detachable Fabric Appliqué

The unusual part of our "temporary" appliqué is that it is removable and reusable. Here's how to easily add an appliqué to any garment—then change it with the seasons or use it on another garment. It's a very versatile accent.

1. Choose your design from a printed fabric or construct your own appliqué using traditional piecing techniques. The fabric for the appliqué may be knit or woven.

2. Back the appliqué with fusible interfacing.

• For knit fabrics, use a knit interfacing like Stacy's Easy Knit.

• For wovens, use a nonwoven interfacing such as Pellon Sof-Shape.

— Appliqué

— Interfacing

3. Cut out the appliqué.

4. Back the appliqué with Stitch-N-Tear to stabilize the design and straightstitch the appliqué to the stabilizer.

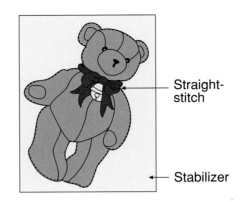

Straight-stitch

Stabilizer

5. Satin-stitch the edges with a narrow zigzag. The "zig" should catch the appliqué, while the "zag" should fall off the edge onto the stabilizer.

• Some of the appliqué's inner features can be highlighted with straight stitching or zigzagging, if desired.

• Remove the Stitch-N-Tear from the back, both outside and inside the stitching line.

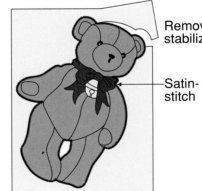

Remove stabilizer.

Satin-stitch

Note from Nancy

Satin-stitching the edges of the appliqué isn't always necessary, since the appliqué will have a glue backing that seals the edges. However, this stitching does provide greater definition and enhances the design.

Timesaving Notions
Making a detachable appliqué with this pressure-sensitive glue is easy! Apply Stikit Again & Again over fabric backed with No-Sew Adhesive. Allow the glue to dry and apply the design to any garment. It also sticks to wood, leather, plastic, glass, metal, and paper. What a great seasonal decorating idea for a child's clothing, room, or windows!

6. Place the appliqué right side down on a layer of waxed paper and seal the back of the fabric with a fabric glue such as No-Sew Adhesive. Apply a thin coat, spreading it evenly with a piece of cardboard.

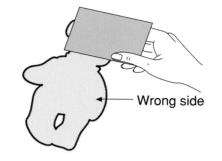

— Wrong side

Allow the glue to dry for several hours.

Note from Nancy
If applied too heavily, fabric glue may bleed through to the right side of the appliqué. Bleed-through is less likely to show if you are using a patterned or heavyweight fabric.

7. After the fabric glue has thoroughly dried, apply a layer of a pressure-sensitive "sticky glue" such as Stikit Again & Again to the back of the appliqué. Distribute the glue evenly over the fabric.
- Allow the glue to dry thoroughly (about eight hours). After the glue has dried, the appliqué can be applied to any garment.
- To launder the garment or to use the appliqué on another garment, simply peel off the appliqué.

Note from Nancy
An easy way to store the appliqué between uses is to place it on an appliqué pressing sheet or between two pieces of waxed paper. When stored properly, the appliqué will remain sticky for many wearings. If the adhesive loses its effect, simply apply another coat of Stikit Again & Again.

Ultrasuede Appliqué

In the *Sewing With Nancy* series "Designer Duplicates," I demonstrated how to borrow designer details from expensive ready-to-wear. Both the original jacket on the right (with a price tag of $250) and the duplicate jacket on the left (much less expensive!) feature confetti-like Ultrasuede appliqués scattered over the shoulders and lapels. The look is smart and the sewing is simple. Here's how!

Note from Nancy
Ultrasuede, the ultimate in luxury, can be cared for with conventional laundering or dry cleaning. Although yardage is expensive, Ultrasuede is available in 9" x 12" designer cuts or in scrap bags at your favorite retail or mail-order outlet.

1. Partially construct the jacket before adding the Ultrasuede "confetti" appliqués.
- Stitch the jacket shoulder seams.
- Attach the under collar to the jacket.
- Set in the sleeves, but do not stitch the sleeve or jacket underarm seams.
- Stitch the front facing to the back facing. Do not stitch the facings to the jacket.

2. Create the confetti appliqués from Ultrasuede.

 • Trace or draw the confetti shapes on the paper side of Wonder-Under. Fuse the fusible web to the wrong side of the Ultrasuede. Cut out the shapes.

Note from Nancy

If you are using Ultrasuede scraps, simply cut the confetti shapes utilizing all the suede sections. Arrange the pieces like a puzzle on a section of Wonder-Under to use all the fusible web and Ultrasuede. Cover with an appliqué pressing sheet. Fuse the Wonder-Under to the wrong side of the Ultrasuede and then cut out the shapes.

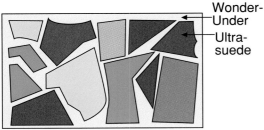

Wonder-Under
Ultra-suede

 • Peel away the paper backing from the Wonder-Under.

3. Fuse the appliqué sections to the jacket.

 • Pin the Ultrasuede appliqués to the jacket and the facing. Pin the facing to the jacket in the position it will be stitched. Try on the jacket and check the position of the appliqués. Move the appliqué pieces, if necessary.

Jacket front

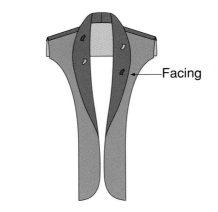

Facing

 • Cover the appliqué pieces with a damp press cloth and fuse.

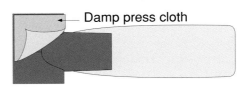

Damp press cloth

Setting Up the Machine for Ultrasuede Appliqué

1. Insert a new sharp sewing needle, size 90/14, in the machine.

2. Use monofilament nylon thread in the needle and thread that matches the fabric in the bobbin. This eliminates the need to change thread color.

3. Adjust the machine for a straightstitch of medium length and stitch around each appliqué. Or, for a hand-stitched look, use a machine-blindhem stitch for this final stitching.

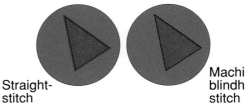

Straight-stitch

Machine blindhem stitch

Timesaving Notions

Another option for positioning appliqués prior to stitching is Liqui-Fuse, a liquid iron-on adhesive that bonds fabrics using heat and moisture. I need to press only once, and the appliqué is securely positioned. (Always test it on a sample before using it on a garment.)

 • *Set the iron to "wool" (no steam).*

 •*Using your finger, spread the liquid fusible web in a thin layer on the wrong side of the appliqué.*

 • *Position the Ultrasuede pieces on the right side of the jacket.*

 • *Cover the Ultrasuede with a press cloth to avoid scorching. Press for three to five seconds to temporarily position the Ultrasuede on the garment.*

 There are other uses for this product. Check the bottle for complete instructions.

Cutwork Appliqué

A favorite *Sewing With Nancy* technique is cutwork appliqué. It combines two sewing techniques and two transferring steps: one for the outer design and the second for the inner cutwork areas. The look is elegant and the sewing is fun!

For the best results, select a solid-colored linen or linen-like fabric. Use tone-on-tone for sophisticated elegance, choosing the same color for both the base fabric and the appliqué. If you prefer a more dominant accent, choose a contrasting color for the cutwork appliqué.

1. Choose a design with open areas for the cutwork appliqué. The design openings must be relatively small so that the open areas will retain their shape.

Note from Nancy
Don't be restricted to conventional cutwork or appliqué designs. Look for design ideas from nontraditional sources such as quilting books, greeting cards, or stationery. The cutwork design on this garment was inspired by a stationery design and was enlarged by using a photocopier.

2. Transfer the appliqué design to the project.
- Trace the *outer outline* of the appliqué design onto the paper side of the Wonder-Under.
- Fuse the Wonder-Under-backed design to the *wrong* side of the appliqué fabric.

- Cut out the outer outline of the appliqué design.
- Remove the paper backing from the Wonder-Under.

Remove paper backing.

- Position the appliqué on the garment, cover with a press cloth, and fuse the appliqué to the garment.

3. Transfer the cutwork areas to the appliqué.

• Place a layer of tulle (bridal veiling or netting) or a sheet of transfer rice paper from a Fabric Pattern Transfer Kit over the original design. Using a fabric marking pen, trace the inner designs.

• Place the tulle or rice paper over the appliqué, aligning the outer outline with the appliqué. Using a fabric marking pen, trace over the lines indicating the cutout areas. The design will transfer to the fabric.

Place rice paper over fused appliqué; trace.

• Cut out the inner shape with an embroidery or appliqué scissors, cutting through both the garment and the appliqué fabric at the same time.

4. Stabilize the design to retain the shape of the cutwork and prevent puckering while stitching.

• Add a layer of Wash-Away plastic stabilizer to the back of a *washable* cutwork section. Or spread a thin layer of Perfect Sew liquid stabilizer on the back and let it

dry. (Always try a small test swatch of fabric with Perfect Sew to be sure you are satisfied with the results.)

> ***Note from Nancy***
> *When I use Perfect Sew, I often use a hair dryer to speed the drying process rather than waiting for the stabilizer to air dry. The Perfect Sew dries in seconds, and I can continue with my project quickly.*

• For nonwashable fabrics, add a layer of Stitch-N-Tear.

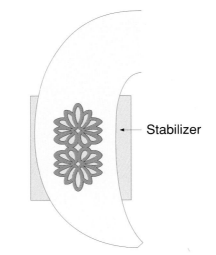

Stabilizer

5. Satin-stitch the outer and inner edges of the cutwork appliqué.

Setting Up the Machine for Cutwork Appliqué

1. Insert a size 90/14 needle. The larger needle reduces the possibility that the embroidery thread will fray and break during stitching.

2. Use cotton or rayon embroidery thread in the needle. For a special accent, you may wish to use metallic thread. In the bobbin, use a lightweight two-ply thread such as Lingerie/Bobbin Thread.

3. Adjust the machine for a zigzag stitch of medium width and short (satin-stitch) length.

4. Loosen the top tension to the buttonhole setting. (Usually this means reducing the tension by two settings.)

5. Replace the presser foot with an embroidery or open toe foot. The foot's large opening makes it easier to see the stitching, helping to improve the appearance of the stitches.

Stitching Cutwork Appliqué

After the appliqué is fused to the garment and backed with a stabilizer, it's time to use a zigzag stitch to complete a stunning embellishment.

Practice the stitching techniques needed for your project on a scrap of fabric before you stitch on your garment or project.

"Undercover" Cutwork

"Undercover" or reverse cutwork is another appliqué variation. The motif featured in the photo is from a bold print. To avoid having the floral print overpower the garment, the print is placed on the wrong side of the garment, behind the fashion fabric. Only small sections of the flower fabric are selected to show, and the fashion fabric is cut away from those areas.

1. Select a print fabric with specific design features that would make interesting motifs—a tropical floral print, a colorful butterfly print, or a geometric design.

2. Determine the sections of the fabric that will be featured in the finished cutwork.

• On the wrong side of the fabric, use a washable marking pen to outline the parts of the design to be uncovered.

• Cut out the motif in a square or rectangular shape, allowing at least a ½" seam allowance around the edges.

• Zigzag the outer edges of the print fabric to prevent the fabric from raveling.

3. Position the cutwork section on the garment.

• Pin the print cutwork section, right side up, on the right side of the garment. (This placement is for positioning only.)

Hold the garment up to your body to be sure the section is located where you want it to be. Adjust the section until you are pleased with the placement.

• Insert pins through the garment at each corner of the print section. The pins will be your guide for positioning the fabric on the wrong side of the garment.

Mark corners with pins.

Right side

• Move the print section to the wrong side of the garment. With the right side of the print against the wrong side of the garment, align the print section with the pin markings.

Setting Up the Machine for Undercover Cutwork

1. Use a thread color that matches the garment fabric in the top and bobbin of the machine.

2. Adjust the sewing machine for a straightstitch with a short stitch length (15 to 18 stitches per inch). The short stitch length makes it easier to turn corners and follow the edges of the design.

Stitching and Cutting the Undercover Cutwork

1. From the wrong side of the garment, stitch around each design section, allowing a small margin around each of the traced outlines. (This margin will be covered later with satin stitching.)

Note from Nancy

It is important to stitch a few areas and then look at the right side of the garment. Before stitching additional sections, trim the stitched areas. If more sections should be exposed, stitch and trim additional sections. Once an area has been cut away, you can't undo it!

2. Cut out the sections to be exposed.

• Turn the garment right side out. The stitched outlines will be visible on the fabric.

• Pinch the center of one of the stitched outlines and carefully pull the outer fabric away from the print fabric. Using an embroidery or appliqué scissors, carefully nip only the outer fabric so that it can be removed.

• Carefully trim the garment fabric inside the stitched outline. If you are using an appliqué scissors, hold the bill of the scissors downward to prevent cutting the print fabric. With a conventional scissors, bevel the blades so that the blades are flat against the outer fabric.

3. Satin-stitch around the cut edges.

• Thread the needle with embroidery thread, metallic thread, or other specialty thread.

• Adjust the machine for a close zigzag stitch of medium width and short length.

• Place a stabilizer on the wrong side of the garment, under the design section. Experiment with a small sample to see which stabilizer works best.

• Satin-stitch around the cut edges of the motif on the right side of the garment.

Note from Nancy
If the outer fabric is fleece, you could eliminate the satin stitching around the outer edges of the cut designs. Just stitch the outline and trim the outer fabric. After laundering, the cut edges will become fuzzy, creating an interesting texture and detail. It's another option!

Traditional Cutwork with Richelieu

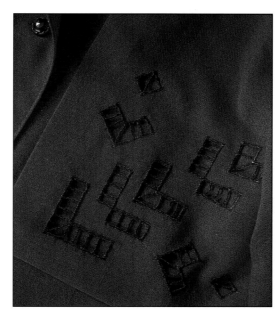

Unlike cutwork appliqué, traditional cutwork is stitched on a single layer of fabric and involves free-motion stitching, cutaway accents, and special satin stitching called Richelieu in the cutout areas. It is a delicate accent for collars, lapels, pockets, and flaps.

For tone-on-tone elegance, use embroidery thread matched to the color of the fabric. For a bolder look, try contrasting thread.

1. Prepare the Richelieu design.

• Choose a simple design. A few cutwork accents strategically placed are more effective than many randomly scattered areas.

• Allow at least ½" of space between sections of the cutwork design.

• Trace the pattern piece on which the design will be applied. Try various designs on the pattern copy to find the right one.

• Using a permanent marking pen, trace the cutwork design onto a layer of Wash-Away stabilizer.

Timesaving Notions

A Spring Embroidery Needle has a miniature spring attached to the needle, which prevents the needle from drawing up the fabric and helps eliminate the possibility of skipped stitches. Use it when the sewing machine is set up for free-motion embroidery work. It's an ideal cutwork accessory.

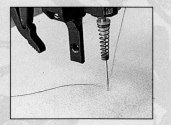

2. Prepare the fabric for cutwork, making a fabric sandwich with the layers in this order:

- A layer of temporary stabilizer.
- The fashion fabric, right side up.
- The stabilizer sheet with the traced cutwork design.

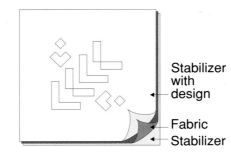

Stabilizer with design

Fabric

Stabilizer

3. Place the sandwich in a machine embroidery hoop.

Note from Nancy

When you are working with an embroidery hoop, the fabric should be large enough to completely fill the hoop. If you are creating a cutwork collar or cuff where the pattern piece is smaller than the hoop area, complete the cutwork first and then cut out the pattern piece.

- Place the outer hoop ring under the fabric sandwich and the inner ring on top.
- Push the inner ring of the hoop into the outer ring, keeping the fabric as taut as possible. The lip of the inner hoop should extend slightly beyond the outer ring.

Note from Nancy

The fabric must be extremely taut inside the hoop—almost like a little drum—so that the completed cutwork will be as smooth as possible. When the inner ring extends beyond the outer one, it creates an extra-taut surface and makes it easier to glide the hoop under the machine.

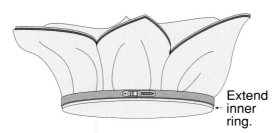

Extend inner ring.

Setting Up the Machine for Richelieu Cutwork

1. Remove the presser foot and disengage the feed dogs. On some machines, you only need to lower or drop the feed dogs. On others, you may need to cover the feed dogs. Check your owner's manual for the proper technique for your machine.

2. Insert a new size 80/12 or 90/14 needle. Or use a size 90 Spring Embroidery Needle.

3. Set your machine for "needle down," if this option is available.

4. Thread the needle and the bobbin of the sewing machine with rayon or cotton embroidery thread.

5. Loosen the thread tension by two settings.

6. Set the machine for a straight stitch. Stitch length is not important since moving the hoop will control the length of the stitches.

Techniques for Richelieu Cutwork

1. Lock the threads.

- Place the hoop under the machine needle. *Lower the presser foot bar.* (If you do not lower the presser bar, the upper thread will be under no tension and the threads will knot and jam on the underside of the fabric instead of making smooth stitches. When you're stitching without a presser foot, it's difficult to tell if the bar has been lowered. Check to be sure!)
- Grasp the top thread. Take one stitch, turning the machine balance wheel by hand to bring the bobbin thread to the top of the fabric.

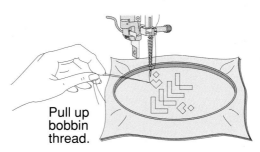

Pull up bobbin thread.

- Hold the top and bobbin threads taut. Turn the balance wheel by hand two or three additional times to secure the stitches. Clip the thread tails.

2. Stitch the traditional cutwork.

• Straightstitch around each design three times. Run the machine at a moderate to fast rate, moving the hoop slowly and evenly so that the stitches are close together.

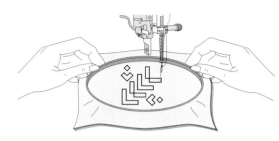

• Cut away the fabric and top stabilizer within the outline areas. If the bottom stabilizer is accidentally trimmed, place a new layer on the bottom without taking the fabric out of the hoop. This avoids disturbing the design.

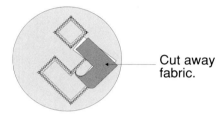

Cut away fabric.

3. Finish the Richelieu cutwork.

• Straightstitch across the cutout areas, beginning and ending in the fashion fabric.

• Stitch from side to side, going over each line three times.

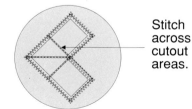

Stitch across cutout areas.

• Change the machine setting to a narrow zigzag stitch. Zigzag over the Richelieu straight stitching.

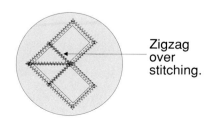

Zigzag over stitching.

• Zigzag around the outer edges of the cutwork. Move the hoop slowly, following the design.

• Remove the fabric from the embroidery hoop and remove the stabilizer.

Other Designer Touches

Charted Needlework Appliqué

Adding charted needlework to a project can be relaxing—almost addictive at times! It's a great way to add a tasteful design to a garment. The unique three-dimensional effect is achieved by satin-stitching over tiny knitting needles. It looks great on home decorating projects and children's wear, as well as on garments for the entire family.

Supplies for Charted Needlework

The needles used in charted needlework are thin, 8"-long double-pointed knitting needles with a diameter of 1.25 mm. A package includes five charted needles—an adequate number for completing most simple designs. If your charted needlework design is quite extensive, you may wish to purchase several packages of needles.

The overlays for charted needlework are transparencies that are placed over the charted needlework design and photocopied, providing guidelines for positioning the charted needles. An overlay package contains three 8½" x 11" plastic sheets, one each with vertical, horizontal, and diagonal lines. These sheets may be reused innumerable times.

Simple linear designs are most suited for charted needlework. Look for simple drawings in pattern books for appliqué, quilting, and counted cross-stitch.

Preparing the Design

Before stitching the charted needlework design, prepare the design for sewing.

1. Select one of the three charted needlework overlays to establish the direction for the charted needlework.

• The vertical overlay makes a design appear long and narrow.

• The horizontal overlay makes the design appear short and wide.

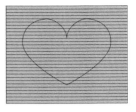

• The diagonal overlay gives the design a feeling of motion.

2. Transfer the overlay lines to the design.

• Position the overlay on top of the design, aligning the marked lines on the overlay with the lines of the design.

• Make a composite photocopy of the design and overlay. Pin the photocopy to the project and use it as a guide in positioning the charted needles.

3. If the original design contains curved lines, convert the curves to straight lines.

• As close to the original line as possible, draw a cross mark on the photocopy at the starting and stopping points for each curved line. This provides guidelines for stitching and keeps the design flowing.

Note from Nancy

You must mark the length of each row of charted needlework stitching to prevent the design from looking out of proportion after it is sewn. It's easy to stitch either too little or too much if the design is not premarked.

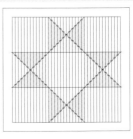

4. Pin or tape the paper charted-needle design to the right side of the fabric. The needlework design is stitched over this paper. When the stitching is completed, any paper that extends beyond the stitched design can be torn away. The charted needlework stitching is very dense; it covers the paper within the design, so the paper will not be visible in the finished project.

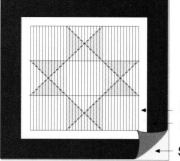

Paper
Fabric
Stabilizer

5. Back the fashion fabric with a stabilizer in the charted-needle design area so that the stitches remain flat and do not pucker.

Setting Up the Machine for Charted Needlework

Much of the setup for charted needlework is similar to that for cutwork. The right setup is the key to this entire technique.

1. Insert a new size 90/14 sewing machine needle. This larger needle withstands the occasional nicking of a charted needle during stitching. Also, using a new needle for each project reduces the likelihood of snags or distorted stitches that may be caused by a dull needle.

2. Use an embroidery or decorative thread in the needle. In the bobbin, use a light-weight thread such as #60 cotton thread, two-ply serger thread, or Lingerie/Bobbin thread.

3. Loosen the upper tension to the buttonhole setting (about two settings).

4. Remove the presser foot, as charted needlework is done free-motion. The fabric will be guided back and forth by hand through the machine as the machine stitches over the needles.

5. Disengage the feed dogs.

6. Adjust the machine for a zigzag stitch of medium width.

7. Do a test run on a scrap of fabric before stitching on the garment. (The stitch length does not require adjustment, since the feed dogs will not guide the fabric through the machine.)

• Place a small portion of the design over a scrap of stabilizer-backed fabric. Place the fabric under the presser foot and bring up the bobbin thread.

• Place a charted needle over the design, aligning it with one of the marked lines on the design.

• Lower the presser bar. Turn the machine balance wheel by hand, carefully watching the machine needle as the zigzag stitch forms. The objective is to have the stitch width as close to the size of the charted needle as possible. The needle should "dance" over the charted needle so that it barely clears it, yet does not hit it.

Charted Needlework Techniques

1. Place the fabric and the design under the presser foot area.

2. *Lower the presser bar.* It's easy to forget this step, but it's extremely important. If the bar isn't lowered, there is no tension on the thread, and the stitching will loop and pucker.

Lower presser bar.

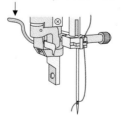

3. Place a charted needle along the first line of the design, working from left to right.

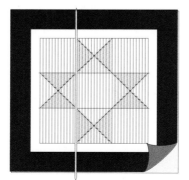

4. Grasp the top thread. Take one stitch, turning the machine balance wheel by hand to bring the bobbin thread to the top of the fabric.

5. Hold the top and the bobbin threads taut. Turn the balance wheel by hand two or three additional times to secure the stitches. Clip the thread tails.

6. Baste the charted needle into position on the design.

• Hold the charted needle in place and zigzag slowly, moving the fabric away from you. Stitches should be approximately ¼" apart.

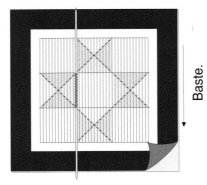

Baste.

• At the end of the row, stop with the needle down in the fabric.

7. Satin-stitch over the basted needle.

• Move the fabric slowly toward you so that the stitches are close together and completely cover the metal on the needle.

• Stop sewing at the end of the design row, with the needle down in the fabric and at the right side of the zigzag stitch. Do not remove the needle from the fabric.

Note from Nancy
If some areas of the charted needlework are not adequately filled in, continue satin-stitching, moving the fabric back and forth until all of the areas are covered.

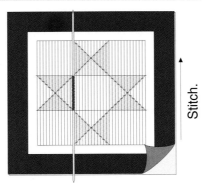

Stitch.

8. Repeat steps to stitch additional rows.

• Place a second needle next to the first and raise the sewing machine needle over the second charted needle. Turn the balance wheel by hand and take several stitches to secure the second charted needle.

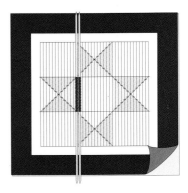

• Repeat the basting and satin-stitching steps. As you add more needles to the design, you need to be a little more careful where you stitch so that you don't accidentally hit one of the needles.

• Do not remove a charted needle from the design until it is needed for another line in the design. Then remove and reuse the needles one at a time, beginning with the first one inserted.

Note from Nancy
It is especially important to keep a charted needle in the row next to the row you are currently stitching. If you don't, the design will be flattened, and you will lose the raised effect of the needlework.

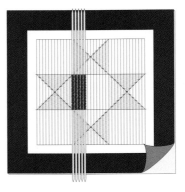

• Repeat the process, positioning and stitching over additional needles until all the rows of one color of the design are completed.

9. To change the colors:

• Reinsert charted needles in the rows where a second color is needed.

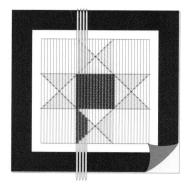

• Clip the top thread next to the fabric. *Do not* clip the bobbin thread or remove the fabric from the sewing machine. By following this sewing order, it is not necessary to bring up the bobbin thread and tie off threads with each color change.

• Thread the top of the machine with the second color. Stitch each row of the second color, inserting and stitching over needles as detailed above.

• Repeat the process for additional colors.

10. Remove the stabilizer and the paper pattern from the project.

Charted Needlework Without Overlays

If you'd like to get a taste of charted needlework before buying overlays, here's a way of adapting the technique.

1. Trace a linear design on a nonwoven or water-soluble stabilizer.

2. Mark a few key lines on the design to aid in keeping the charted needles straight during stitching.

3. Position the charted needles next to each other, using the marked lines to keep the design straight, and stitch the design.

Charted Needlework from Counted Cross-stitch Designs

Counted cross-stitch patterns are naturals for charted needlework. The cross-stitch pattern is already gridded, providing lines for positioning the charted needles. Gridded cross-stitch designs are suitable for either horizontal or vertical needle placement.

1. Photocopy the original cross-stitch pattern. (Retain the original to check that the design lines are not changed during stitching.)

2. Use a washable marking pen to highlight the various sections of the design and to provide a guide for changing thread colors.

3. Tape the photocopied cross-stitch design to the project. Stitch with charted needles.

Timesaving Notions
I like using a serger tweezers to remove any paper fragments from the stitches after doing the charted needlework. The tweezers reach even the smallest pieces of paper.

Machine Quilting

Add a layer of quilt batting to the back of a fabric and then further enhance the fabric's appearance by outlining motifs with free-motion machine stitching. This combination of quilting and machine embroidery adds a sophisticated raised effect.

1. Trace the design onto the right side of the fabric. (Begin with a larger fabric square or rectangle than needed. The stitching slightly draws in the fabric.)

2. Back the fabric with one or two layers of batting.

3. Center the fabric and batting in a machine embroidery hoop.

Machine Setup for Free-Motion Embroidery

These are the general steps for the sewing machine setup and locking the threads for free-motion embroidery. For more specific directions, refer to pages 127 to 129 under "Traditional Cutwork with Richelieu."

1. Lower the feed dogs to the darning position and remove the presser foot.

2. Loosen the top tension by two settings. Attach a Spring Embroidery Needle (optional).

3. Thread the needle with machine embroidery thread such as Sulky. Use lightweight Lingerie/Bobbin thread in the bobbin to reduce thread buildup on the wrong side of the fabric.

4. Adjust the machine for a straight stitch.

5. Lock the threads. Place the hoop and fabric under the presser foot.
- Lower the presser bar.
- Draw up the bobbin thread and stitch several stitches in place to lock the threads. Clip the excess thread tails.

Quilting Techniques

1. Run the machine at a moderate to fast rate and move the hoop in a tight circular motion to make a "squiggle stitch."

2. Move the hoop at an even pace, following the outline of the design. The faster you sew, the easier it is to work with the design.

3. Create squiggle-stitch designs outside or inside the design area. The motif area of the design will have a raised effect due to the layers of batting.

4. Raise the presser foot and remove the hoop from the machine when the stitching is completed. Clip the threads.

Serger Appliqué

Attention, serger owners! Using either the overlock or rolled-edge stitch, you can create interesting appliqué variations with your serger. There are many types of threads available—experiment with several for attractive effects.

Serger appliqué works best on knit fabrics. Knits are easier to maneuver under the serger, and you don't have to worry about raveling. To provide stability, knits should be backed with fusible interfacing. Simple geometric shapes are perfect choices for serged appliqué designs.

Serger Appliqué Basics

1. Back the knit fabrics with a fusible knit interfacing such as Knit Shape.

2. Trace and cut out the appliqué design.

Setting Up the Serger for Appliqué

1. For a wide serged edge, adjust the serger settings for a 3-thread overlock stitch, using only the left needle. For a narrow edge on the appliqué, set the serger for a rolled-edge stitch.

2. Use a decorative thread in the upper looper. Possibilities include Decor 6 thread, Ribbon Floss, pearl cotton, and Sulky rayon embroidery thread.

3. Use ThreadFuse in the lower looper. (If ThreadFuse is not available, use basic serger thread.)

4. In the needle, use basic serger thread that matches the color of the upper looper thread.

5. Test the stitch on a scrap of fabric for the correct tension setting.

Serge the Appliqué

1. Serge the appliqué edges. Apply a drop of Fray Check or No Fray to seal the stitches and prevent raveling at the ends of the stitching. Allow the sealant to dry thoroughly.

2. Position and fuse the appliqué to the garment.

• If ThreadFuse was used in the lower looper, fuse-baste the appliqué to the garment by pressing over the appliqué.

• If serger thread was used in the lower looper, fuse narrow strips of Wonder-Under to the wrong side of the appliqué along the outer edges. Remove the paper backing and fuse the appliqué in place.

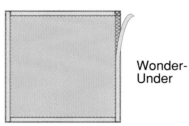

Wonder-Under

3. Topstitch the appliqué to the garment, using a conventional sewing machine.

Sewing Basics

PATTERN BASICS

Pattern Envelope

Much helpful information is printed on the pattern envelope, including:

- *Photos or sketches* that show all the variations of the style included in the pattern.
- *Illustrations* that show the back view of the garment.
- *Body Measurement/Yardage Chart* that helps determine the amount of fabric and interfacing to purchase.
- *Suggested Fabrics* list that guides fabric selection.
- *Notions* list that details the buttons, snaps, hooks and eyes, zippers, elastic, and thread required to make the garment.

Guide Sheet

The guide sheet also contains valuable information, including:

- Illustrations of all pattern pieces for the different pattern views.
- An explanation of symbols and terms used on the pattern pieces.
- Basic information on interfacing, pattern adjustments, cutting, marking, and sewing the garment.
- Illustrations of cutting layouts that show how to place the pattern pieces on the fabric.
- Step-by-step instructions and illustrations showing how to make the project.

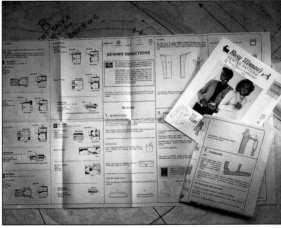

Tissue Patterns

The tissue patterns have a variety of symbols printed directly on them, including:

- *Cutting line*—a solid, dark outer line, often with scissors sketches to indicate the cutting line.
- *Stitching line*—a broken line drawn ⅝", ⅜", or ¼" inside the cutting line to indicate where to sew.
- *Grain line arrow*—used to help align the pattern on the fabric. Position the printed arrow parallel to the grain (usually lengthwise) of the fabric.

- *Fold line*—a thinner solid line to be placed on the fold of the fabric. A second parallel line with a double-ended arrow points to the fold line, and the words "Place on fold" may appear by the line.
- *Notches*—single or double diamonds with corresponding numbers to help match garment pieces accurately when sewing.
- *Circles and squares*—additional marks that help align and match garment pieces more precisely. They may also indicate points at which to start or stop stitching.
- *Hemline, center front and back, and fold line*—show placement of construction details. "Lengthen or shorten here" lines show positions for lengthening or shortening a pattern length without changing the lines or the fit of the garment.

LAYOUT & CUTTING TIPS

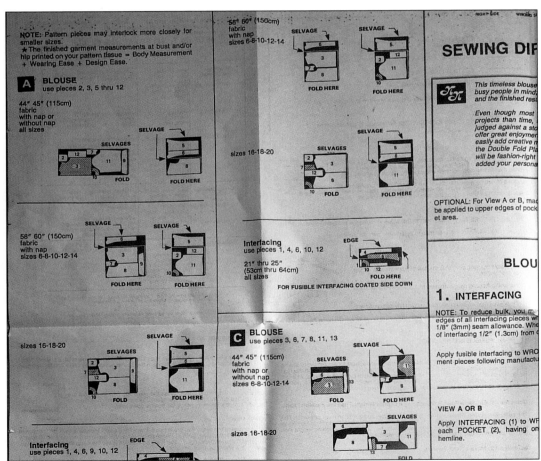

1. Cut out the tissue pieces you need and return the others to the envelope.

2. Press the pattern pieces with a warm, dry iron to remove any wrinkles that might distort the shape of the pattern pieces when you cut out the garment.

3. Using the correct pattern layout from the guide sheet, position the larger pieces on the fabric first.

4. For each, locate the grain line arrow and pin one end to the fabric. Measure the distance from that end of the arrow to the fabric fold or selvage. Repeat for the other end of the arrow. Both distances must be the same. Pivot the pattern until the two distances are equal. Pin the second arrow end.

5. If a pattern piece has a "Place on fold" line, place that line exactly on the fold of the fabric. Pin the pattern along the fold. Insert a pin diagonally in each corner of the pattern pieces. Use extra pins around curved areas and place pins every 6" to 8" along the cutting line (parallel to, but not on, the line).

6. Position smaller pattern pieces on the fabric and pin.

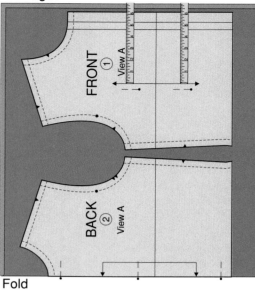

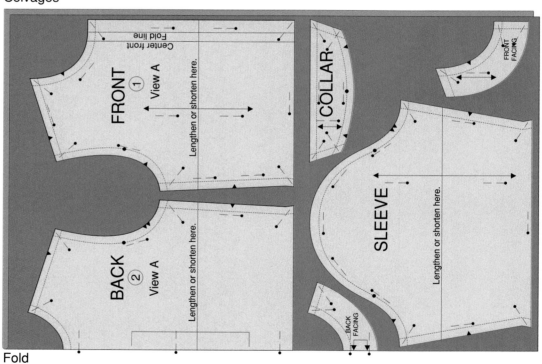

SEAMS

Seams are the foundation element for successful sewing. Here are some seam basics:

1. With right sides together, align the notches and the cut edges of the garment pieces.

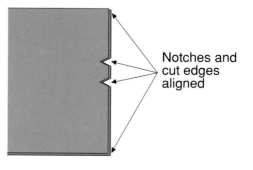

Notches and cut edges aligned

2. When sewing with a conventional machine, insert pins perpendicular to the edge of the fabric, with the points in and the heads toward the fabric's cut edge. (If you are using a serger, position pins parallel to the seam and 1" from the cut edge so that the blades are not damaged by the pins.)

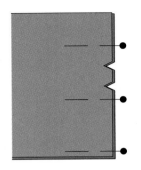

3. Begin and end each seam by locking the stitches. Sew two or three stitches with the stitch length set at "0" (or the shortest length available).

4. Adjust the stitch length to 10 to 12 stitches per inch (the normal setting) for the rest of the seam.

5. Stitch in the direction of the grain line. Sewing from the widest to the narrowest part of the garment is frequently referred to as "directional stitching." Directional stitching is recommended because the machine is sewing with the grain of the fabric; stitching against the grain can cause the fabric to stretch or pucker.

6. Remove pins as you come to them to avoid breaking your sewing machine needle or serger knife.

FINISHING SEAMS

It is important to finish seams to prevent fraying, especially if the garment will be machine-laundered. The seam is flatter and neater if the seam finishes are done on a single thickness of fabric. Here are some recommended ways to finish seams.

• Zigzag over the cut edges. Adjust the machine for a zigzag stitch with a medium width and a medium-to-short stitch length. Stitch the "zig" in the fabric and the "zag" off the cut edge, holding the raw edge taut while you zigzag to prevent the edge from curling.

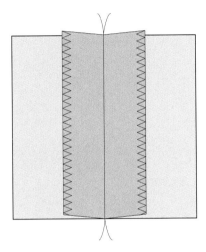

• Serge the edges with a 3-thread or 3/4-thread overlock stitch. This is the newest, fastest, and neatest seam finish available to home sewers.

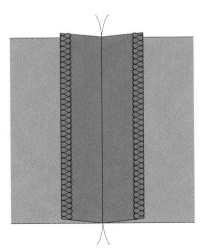

• Trim the edges with pinking shears. Pinking is perfect for lightweight, tightly constructed fabrics such as silk and silk-like fabrics.

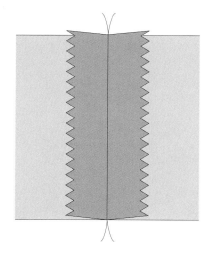

• French seams are the perfect choice for woven fabrics, especially for sheer, light-weight fabrics. It encases the raw edges and produces an attractive seam.

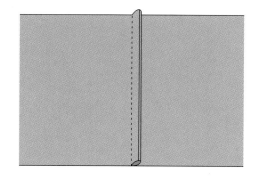

DURABLE DARTS

Darts, triangular folds with wide ends tapering to a point, help shape a garment so that it fits around body contours. A smooth and durable dart can be sewn quickly using the following steps:

1. With your scissors, nip the dart's stitch-ing lines at the cut edge. On the wrong side of the garment, mark the point of the dart with a pin.

2. Fold the dart with right sides together, matching the nip markings at the cut edge.

3. Place the cut edge of the fabric under the presser foot and lower the needle but do not lower the presser foot.

4. Pull the top thread to form an 8" to 12" thread tail. Lower the presser foot and lay

the thread on top of the fabric, angling it toward the pin mark. This will mark the stitching line between the nips and the point of the dart.

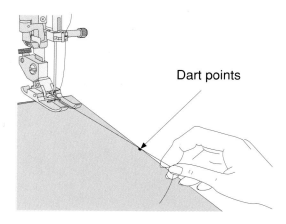

Dart points

5. Stitch in place several times to lock the stitching. Lengthen the stitch to normal length and, using the thread as a guide, finish stitching the dart.

6. At the end of the dart, turn the machine's wheel by hand, barely catching three to four stitches along the fold.

7. Stitch off the fabric 1" to 2", forming a chain of thread. Secure the chained thread tail by sewing two or three stitches in place in the dart. Trim the thread ends.

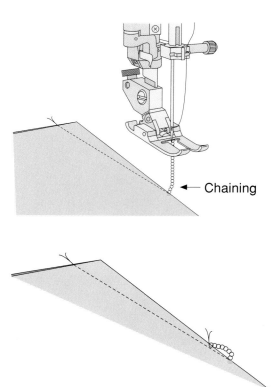

Chaining

GATHERING METHODS

This method for gathering fabric is quicker than the two rows of basting stitches recommended on pattern guide sheets.

1. Place the fabric under the presser foot. Turn the wheel by hand to take one complete stitch in the fabric and bring up the bobbin thread by lightly pulling on the top thread. Pull the bobbin thread to the top side.

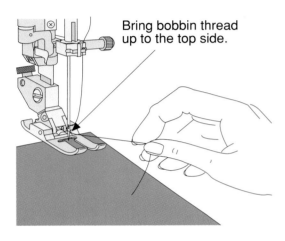

Bring bobbin thread up to the top side.

2. Pull the bobbin and top threads to measure as long as the area to be gathered. Gently twist the two threads together.

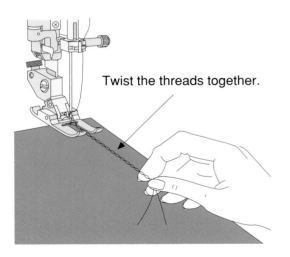

Twist the threads together.

3. Set your machine for a wide zigzag stitch and a short stitch length. Zigzag over the twisted threads inside the seam allowance, making a "casing" for the gathering threads. Do not stitch through the twisted threads.

Zigzag over threads.

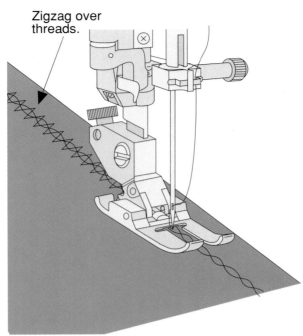

4. Gather by pulling the twisted threads. The gathering threads will not pull out of the fabric, because the threads are anchored in the first stitch. Adjust the gathers and attach to the garment following the pattern guide sheet.

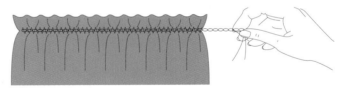

*N*ancy Zieman— businesswoman, home economist, and national sewing authority—is the producer and hostess of the popular show *Sewing With Nancy,* which appears exclusively on public television stations. The show, broadcast since September 1982, is the longest-airing sewing program on television. Nancy organizes each show in a how-to format, concentrating on step-by-step instructions.

Nancy also produces and hosts *Sewing With Nancy* videos. Each video contains three segments from her television program. Currently, there are twenty-eight one-hour videos being used by retailers, educators, libraries, and sewing groups.

In addition, Nancy is founder and president of Nancy's Notions Sewing Catalog. This large catalog contains more than 4,000 products, including sewing books, notions, videos, and fabrics.

Nancy has written six books: *The Busy Woman's Sewing Book* and *The Busy Woman's Fitting Book* with Robbie Fanning, the *Slacks Fitting Book, Let's Sew!, 10-20-30 Minutes to Sew,* and *The Best of Sewing With Nancy.* In each book, Nancy emphasizes efficient sewing techniques that produce professional results.

Nancy was named the 1988 Entrepreneurial Woman of the Year by The Wisconsin Women Entrepreneurs Association. In 1991, she also received the National 4-H Alumni Award. She is a member of the American Home Economics Association and the American Home Sewing & Craft Association.

Nancy lives in Beaver Dam, Wisconsin, with her husband/business partner, Rich, and their two sons, Ted and Tom.